IMAGES
of America

SQUIRREL HILL

This *c.* 1890 photograph shows sheep on the Hasley farm, located on the eastern edge of Squirrel Hill. Within 20 years, this area began to be residentially subdivided. Additional pictures of this farm have been included in this book.

IMAGES
of America

SQUIRREL HILL

Squirrel Hill Historical Society

ARCADIA
PUBLISHING

Published by Arcadia Publishing
Charleston, South Catolina

Library of Congress Catalog Card Number: 2004117444

For all general information contact Arcadia Publishing at:
Telephone 843-853-2070
Fax 843-853-0044
E-mail sales@arcadiapublishing.com
For customer service and orders:
Toll-Free 1-888-313-2665

Visit us on the Internet at www.arcadiapublishing.com

The Forbes Avenue retail area is shown in a view looking east from Murray Avenue to Shady Avenue in 1930. This remains one of Pittsburgh's most vibrant neighborhood commercial corridors today.

CONTENTS

ACKNOWLEDGMENTS

Betty Connelly and Laurie Cohen edited this book and wrote significant sections of the text.

Michael Ehrmann, chairman of the Squirrel Hill Historical Society (SSHS), coordinated the search for photographs included in this volume and also wrote several of the chapters. SSHS members Patti Hughes, Ralph Lund, Esther Tucker, Sanford Baskind, and Mark Iskovitz all made important contributions to this work.

A primary photographic source for this book is the Arthur Smith Collection of Chatham College, located in Squirrel Hill. Elisabeth Roark, associate professor of art at Chatham College, offered us access to this collection and also to selected Chatham College Collection photographs and descriptions.

Other major photographic contributors include the Pittsburgh Parks Conservancy, which also provided significant historical material on the parks and helped identify individual photographs; the Pittsburgh Board of Education, which allowed us to use photographs never before shared with other organizations and provided major historical material on the Squirrel Hill schools; the Carnegie Library of Pittsburgh Pennsylvania Collection; and Raymond Hasley. The family of Raymond Hasley operated the Hasley farm, which was later subdivided into a number of Squirrel Hill residential blocks. The family also owned a construction company that built the early phases of the Homewood Cemetery and the Pittsburgh Country Club, among many other projects.

Additional contributions were made by the following institutions and individuals: the Rodef Shalom Congregation Archives and Martha Berg; the Sixth Presbyterian Church and David Miller; the Episcopal Church of the Redeemer and SHHS member Marian Cook; Temple Beth Shalom and Rabbi Steven Steindel; Tree of Life Synagogue and Joel Goldstein; Temple Sinai and Phyllis Weinkle; Carriage House Children's Center, Nathalie Kaplan and Myrna Hill; the Mary S. Brown Memorial Methodist Episcopal Church and June Swiger; and the Homewood Cemetery and Marilyn Evert. Melanie Fitzpatrick, Steve Boxsenbaum, John Husack, Stanley Karas Jr., Anita-Kulina Smith, Sylvia Sachs, and Margaret Domer were also helpful. We apologize to anyone not recognized; our thanks go to everyone who contributed in any way to this work.

This pictorial history has been limited by both space and availability of photographs. The early settlers left few images, and only because of space does this book end in the early 1950s with the opening of the Squirrel Hill Tunnel. As a result of these limitations, we do not consider our work to be a full history of the neighborhood. Instead, we hope that the reader will consider this a good introduction to the subject.

INTRODUCTION

Squirrel Hill is one of Pittsburgh's premier residential neighborhoods and also has a vibrant neighborhood commercial center and three exceptional parks. In a time when city neighborhoods across the nation struggle for survival, Squirrel Hill thrives, develops, and redevelops itself.

Location is certainly one factor. The neighborhood attracts students, professors, and researchers who commute to the nearby institutions of higher education and continuously expanding medical-research complexes. Musicians, artists, and a mix of other professionals and blue-collar workers have also been enchanted by the beauty of the area, with its rolling hills, river overlooks, stately streets, restaurants, coffeehouses, shops, and houses of worship. Squirrel Hill is the neighborhood where Gene Kelly taught dancing classes and, more recently, where Fred Rogers (Mr. Rogers) spent a goodly amount of time.

Architectural diversity is another factor. Many of the houses built in Squirrel Hill between 1865 and 2005 were designed by noted architects. Housing styles range from Victorian and Edwardian to Art Deco and Contemporary. The housing price range in the area is just as broad and can accommodate single students as readily as large families, retirees, middle-class folk, and the well-to-do. Living options for senior citizens have also been developed.

Squirrel Hill is noted for having excellent public schools and a variety of private schools. Surrounding parks and many trees in the neighborhood remove the area from its urban confines. All of these factors make Squirrel Hill an exceptional environment in which to live.

The borders most commonly agreed upon for the Squirrel Hill neighborhood are part or all of Schenley Park, Frick Park, the southern side of Fifth Avenue, and the first ridge above the Monongahela River (the Summerset and old Brown's Hill Road areas). The 2000 census counted 24,915 people within the neighborhood's boundaries. History and homesteads, however, did not neatly follow such arbitrary boundaries. The authors of this book have gone beyond the generally recognized boundaries to include some adjacent places that have influenced life in Squirrel Hill.

The Squirrel Hill Historical Society was founded in 2000 to explore and celebrate the history of the neighborhood. The society is a volunteer membership organization. Its primary activity is the sponsorship of monthly meetings with speakers who are knowledgeable about the history of Squirrel Hill and its environs. The society is actively compiling an archive of local historical documents, and this book is an exciting and important step in that mission. You are invited to join the historical society in developing a neighborhood that respects and preserves its history.

One

EARLY SQUIRREL HILL

Squirrel Hill's early settlers were predominantly of English and Scottish descent. The farmers who came next were frequently of German ancestry. Then, as large estates were being built, entrepreneurial Protestants called it their neighborhood.

Compared to the neighboring communities of Oakland and Shadyside, Squirrel Hill was late in being developed. It was wooded and had limited access. There was a lane from Shadyside and another path from Hazelwood (then called Saltworks Road and now called Saline Street). There was a path up the hill from the Monongahela River (now Brown's Hill Road). A major Native American trail, Nemacolin's, crossed the Squirrel Hill ridge. During the Revolutionary War era, it was called Braddock's Road. The trail connected to Four Mile Run (along present-day Saline Street).

Landmarks in the early life of Squirrel Hill were farm paths, hills, streams, and (hard to imagine today) trees. Four tree landmarks have been identified. Until the early 20th century, a magnificent black oak tree stood at one of the early intersections in Squirrel Hill, where Beechwood Boulevard now crosses Forward Avenue. On the Irwin Farm (near Forbes and Murray Avenues today) stood a glorious elm tree whose shade was so dense that rain did not penetrate. This elm covered an area so big that it became a natural gathering place where folks met to celebrate happy times and mourn sad events. Political discussions surely covered the French and Indian War, the Revolutionary War, the Whiskey Tax Rebellion, and the Civil War. Some of the first religious exercises were held there. The elm fell in a storm in 1897.

Another huge tree where pioneers gathered was near Forward Avenue where it is joined by Shady Avenue. When the Peebles Township road was laid (before 1923), the tree was scaled down to five feet. A little farther away (about where Douglas Avenue enters Shady Avenue) stood a grove of maple trees where young men and women gathered to cook gallons of maple sugar. Today Squirrel Hill residents meet and greet around street intersections, such as those at Forbes and Shady Avenues and at Forbes and Murray Avenues.

The early pioneers' homes were scattered, but there is documented activity of three locations. Some centered around present-day Brown's Hill Road and Beechwood Boulevard. The area around Phillips Avenue and Beechwood Boulevard was another area of settlement. The third was Forbes Avenue near Schenley Park. Farms developed northward across the hills toward Oakland and Shadyside.

Even the Native Americans called the area Squirrel Hill. The photographs in this chapter merely hint at the pioneers' history.

In 1769, the first cabin officially recorded in the area was at Summerset on the Monongahela. It belonged to Col. James Burd, who was stationed at Fort Pitt. That year, when the Pennsylvania colony began selling land here, 19 people applied. Some were already settled here; others lived here but did not purchase land at the time. This 1950s view shows that Summerset was used as a slag dump before the area was reclaimed for a housing development known as Summerset at Frick Park.

On the other side of Squirrel Hill, near Phillips Avenue and Beechwood Boulevard, James Fleming built a log cabin in 1775. Fleming, a Scot, marched to Pittsburgh with Stanwix and there opened a store with goods he brought with him. Eventually he owned 314 acres. He died in 1836, leaving a large family and a large estate. This view from his farm is now from Frick Park.

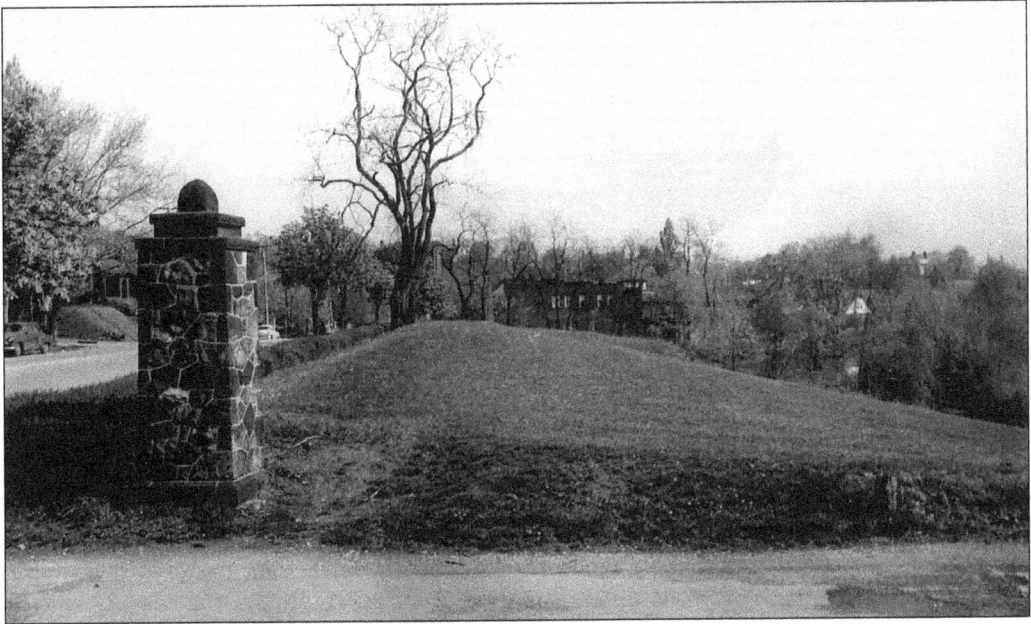

Part of Nemacolin's Trail (later called Braddock's Road and now Beechwood Boulevard) ran through James Fleming's property. His second house, part of which still stood in 1915, was near Pocusset Street and Beechwood Boulevard. Three hundred yards away from there was another Native American trail that led from Braddock's Road to East Liberty. The whole tract was underlaid with coal. For many years, Fleming's grandson mined coal on his farm for commercial and domestic use.

James Fleming had a maple grove later called Fleming's Sugar Camp near Douglas Avenue. A little beyond it was a spring the Native Americans called Sweet Water. Reportedly, a young Scotch maid bringing water to the Fleming family was scalped there. Some streets reflect the names of landowners. English Lane (shown here) was named for Thomas English, a later owner of part of Fleming's property.

11

Where the Fleming Farm adjoined the Irwin Farm (near Shady Avenue and Bartlett Street) was a graveyard used by some pioneer families. Also in this plot were two large Native American mounds, which were not disturbed until the opening of Bartlett Street, when all were removed. This photograph of streets being cut through (in this case, Willard from Dallas) took place about the same time, the late 1800s.

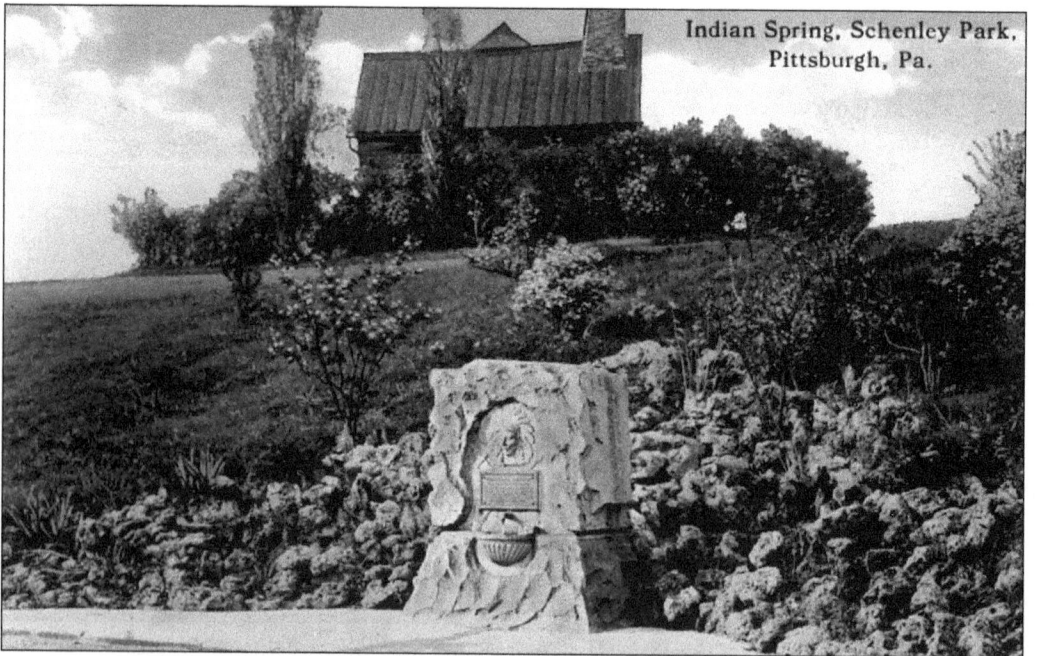

Indian Spring, Schenley Park, Pittsburgh, Pa.

Pioneer David Irwin's home stood near the intersection of Forbes and Murray Avenues. During the era of Native American conflicts, it served as a stockade for seven families until an area truce was declared. Irwin's house is gone, but nearby in Schenley Park is a spring memorializing Catahecassa Blackhoof, Shawnee chief. The Neil Log House is in the background.

The Neil Log House was built between 1769 and 1775. When Schenley Park was given to the city in 1889, there were about a dozen pioneer structures in it. Only two remain. This cabin, now located on the Schenley golf course, was the scene of much merrymaking and was the location of a runaway marriage of two prominent early settlers. It has been restored.

The Martin cabin, on Overlook Drive in Schenley Park, is one of three extant 18th-century buildings in Pittsburgh. Like the Neil house, it had several owners and was put to various uses. It is currently not in use. There is little verifiable daily and social history of the period between 1776 and 1865 for Squirrel Hill.

The Girty-Turner family was the most historically notable and perhaps the earliest of the area's settlers. Simon Girty Sr., an Irish emigrant and trader in central Pennsylvania, married Mary Newton and had four sons—Thomas, Simon, James, and George. After her husband's death, Mary Girty married John Turner and had another son, John Turner Jr. After living through Native American raids, captivity, and another widowhood, the mother and sons were reunited in 1765, and they settled in the Squirrel Hill area. Mary Girty-Turner lived in a log house near Beechwood Boulevard and Hazelwood Avenue. Shown here is the cabin of her son John Turner. Built c. 1778, it was occupied until at least 1929, when this photograph was taken. The cabin was located on Loretta Street near Frank Street.

When Mary Girty-Turner died, she was buried not far away on Turner land. In 1838, two years before he died at 85, John Turner deeded to the community the land that surrounded the graveyard. Turner and his wife, Susanna, were buried there with other early settlers. It was called the Turner Cemetery and is adjacent to the Mary S. Brown Memorial Methodist Episcopal Church, on Beechwood Boulevard.

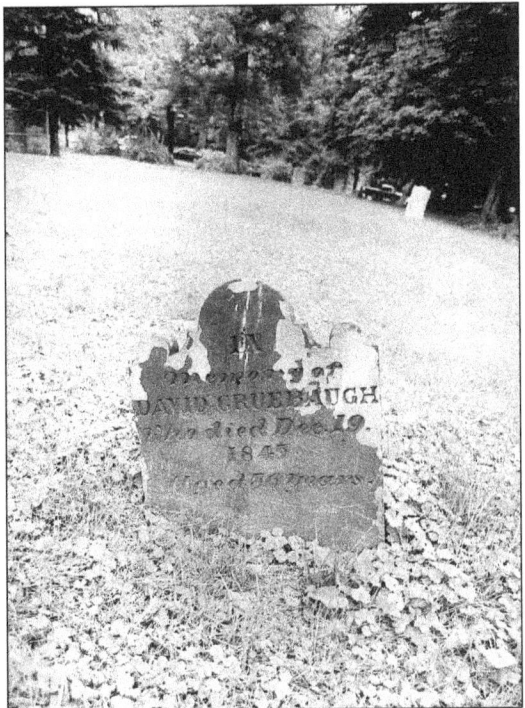

John Turner had considerable land. He purchased 154 acres early and supposedly 19 more tracts. His farm produced well. He knew the needs of Fort Duquesne and planted only those crops that he could sell to the garrison. His land, called Federal Hill, survives as a street name next to the Turner Cemetery. This stone reads, "In memory of David Gruebaugh, who died Dec. 19, 1845, Aged 56 years."

When John Turner deeded the graveyard to the community, some of the early settlers had already been interred there. The earliest burial on record (1804) was that of Mrs. William Craig. The oldest headstones and limestone slabs have crumbled to dust, and preservation is an issue. This stone reads, "William Bell, died July 6, 1851, age 38 years."

John Turner's half-brother, Simon Girty Jr., is noted for fighting during the French and Indian Wars. In the 1930s, when houses were being constructed by the Born Realty Company, a steam shovel uncovered the remains of a log-and-adobe hut that was believed to have been the residence of Simon Girty. This discovery was on Beechwood Boulevard, near the junction with Forward Avenue.

This stone reads, "Samuel Fowkes, a member of Co. K. of 102 Reg. Vt., died March 30, 1863, in the 57th year of his age." Those who took part in several different wars are in the cemetery. Abraham Boother was a Revolutionary War soldier and was buried with the honors of war c. 1830. John Turner took part in different campaigns against the Native Americans. William Craig was a soldier in the War of 1812. Henry Brewno was a soldier in the Mexican War. Many of those buried in the cemetery fought in the Civil War, including William Nelson, John Clark, and Samuel Fowkes. In 1908, Capt W. Harry Brown erected a bronze plaque in the adjacent church with the names of all church members who served as soldiers from 1755 to 1865.

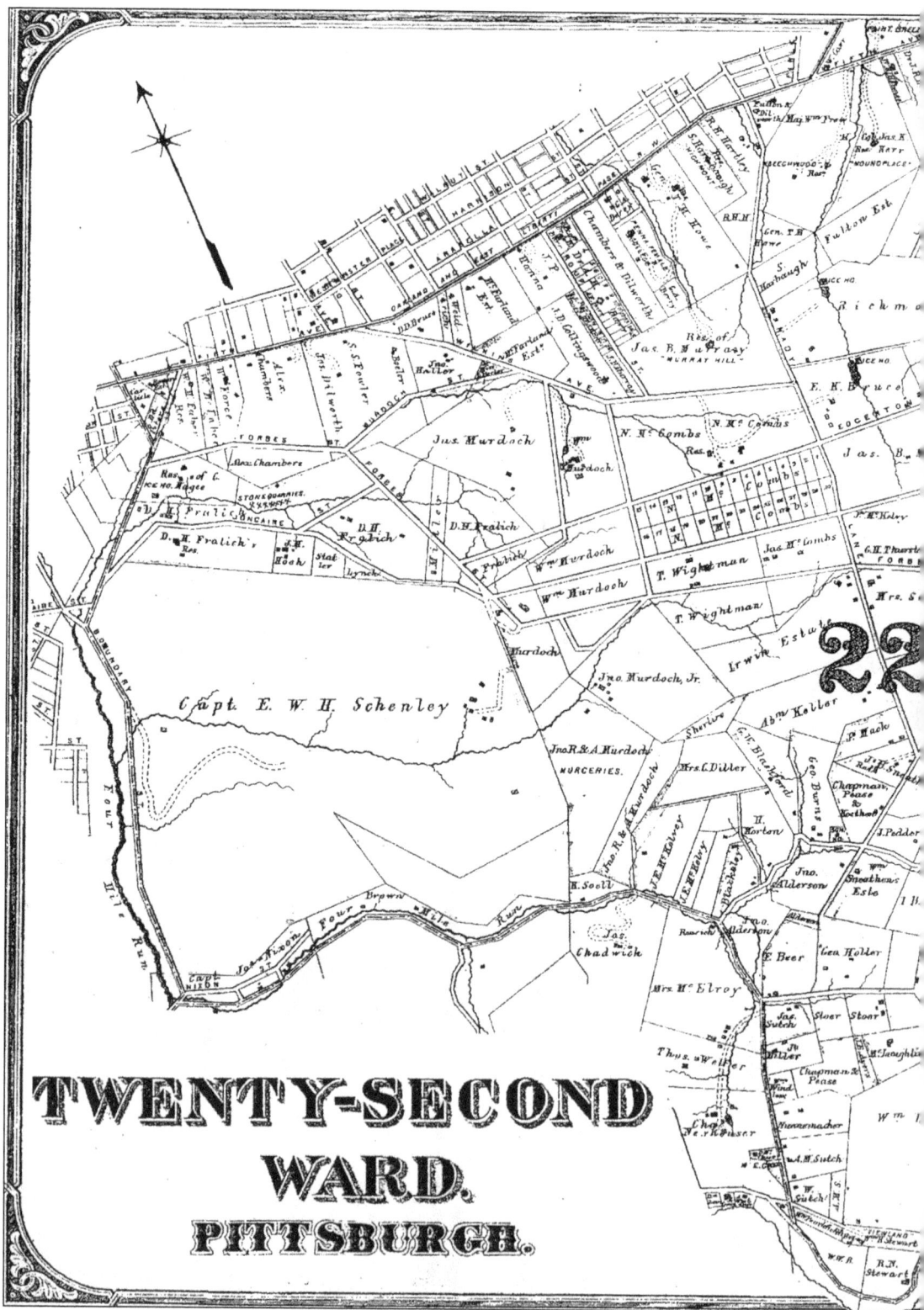

TWENTY-SECOND WARD.
PITTSBURGH.

1872

Liberty Township, which included Squirrel Hill, was incorporated into the rapidly expanding city of Pittsburgh in 1867. It became the 22nd Ward. This map from 1872 shows community landowners and major roads. Notice that the pioneer Fleming Farm is now in the hands of the Phillips, the English, and other families. The Irwin Farm is mostly in the hands of descendants. Thomas Wightman's 10-acre estate and the holdings of the various Murdoch family members are in place. Limited development of small housing lots is shown. The land that would become Schenley Park is listed in the name of the husband of James O'Hara's heir, Mary Croghan Schenley. The road and street names on this map are not exactly as they have come to be today.

19

The last recorded burial in Turner Cemetery is that of Edward Schenly Ebdy, who died in 1880.

In time, land changed hands. Pioneer families intermarried. Over 125 years, the Squirrel Hill neighborhood moved from being sparsely settled by pioneers to being moderately settled by farms. This 1893 photograph of Forward Avenue was taken from Terrace Ridge. Farm gates and lanes are visible. There were still large areas of dense woods, and it was easy to become hopelessly lost while trying to find a route between Negley and Penn Avenues.

Two

FARMS, ESTATES, AND THE HOMEWOOD CEMETERY

Much of Squirrel Hill in the 1800s consisted of farms and undeveloped tracts of land. In the late 1800s, however, a number of executives from the oil and steel companies moved to Squirrel Hill and built massive estates for their families. The early homes of William Thaw, Daniel Clemson, Augustus Frauenheim, John Worthington, and various members of the Mellon family are shown on the pages ahead. These houses often contained ballrooms for dancing, elaborate gardens, and plenty of room for live-in servants.

There were many reasons for the development of Squirrel Hill and surrounding areas as "estate country" during this period. However, the construction of electric trolleys along Forbes and Murray Avenues in 1893 and the gradual development and paving of residential streets during this period clearly contributed to the accelerating trend.

Three homes belonging to the Mellon family are included in this chapter—those of Andrew W. Mellon, Richard Beatty Mellon, and William Larimer Mellon. The only one that remains standing today is that of Andrew W. Mellon, on the Chatham College campus. All three of these men were very influential leaders, both locally and nationally. Andrew W. Mellon served as secretary of the Treasury in three administrations and donated his outstanding art collection, which resulted in the building and furnishing of the National Gallery of Art in Washington, D.C.

Richard Beatty Mellon was Andrew's brother and became president of what was then called Mellon National Bank. He donated the funds for the construction of East Liberty Presbyterian Church on Penn Avenue and laid the cornerstone. William Larimer Mellon founded the Gulf Oil Corporation in 1907 and provided much of the funds for the establishment of the Graduate School of Industrial Administration at Carnegie Mellon University.

The Murdoch family, who owned floral shops downtown and grew flowers in their Squirrel Hill and Oakland greenhouses, owned large tracts of land now known as Murdoch Farms, between Wightman Street and Schenley Park.

The Homewood Cemetery is also included in this chapter. Founded in 1876, it occupies 196 acres of land at the edge of Squirrel Hill, bordering on Point Breeze and Regent Square. Many prominent Pittsburghers have been interred there, including Henry Clay Frick, Henry J. Heinz, Capt. W. Harry Brown, Andrew W. Mellon, and Edward Bigelow. In addition to Civil War graves, mausoleums, and obelisks, there is a Chinese section, complete with an altar and shrine. One section of 19th-century architecture has extensive ironwork, stained glass, and sculptures. The grounds of the cemetery were landscaped in an understated style; in an earlier time, they included a functioning greenhouse and stables on site.

The Hasley farm was located at 6733 Forward Avenue, near English Lane. The Monongahela River was visible from the farm, which is currently part of the Summerset at Frick Park development.

Pigs and chickens were raised on the Hasley farm. Other farms in Squirrel Hill at the beginning of the 20th century included the Beehner, Welfer, and Ninehouser farms.

This is a construction crew from the W. J. Hasley Company. The specific location is not known, but the photograph dates from the 1880s.

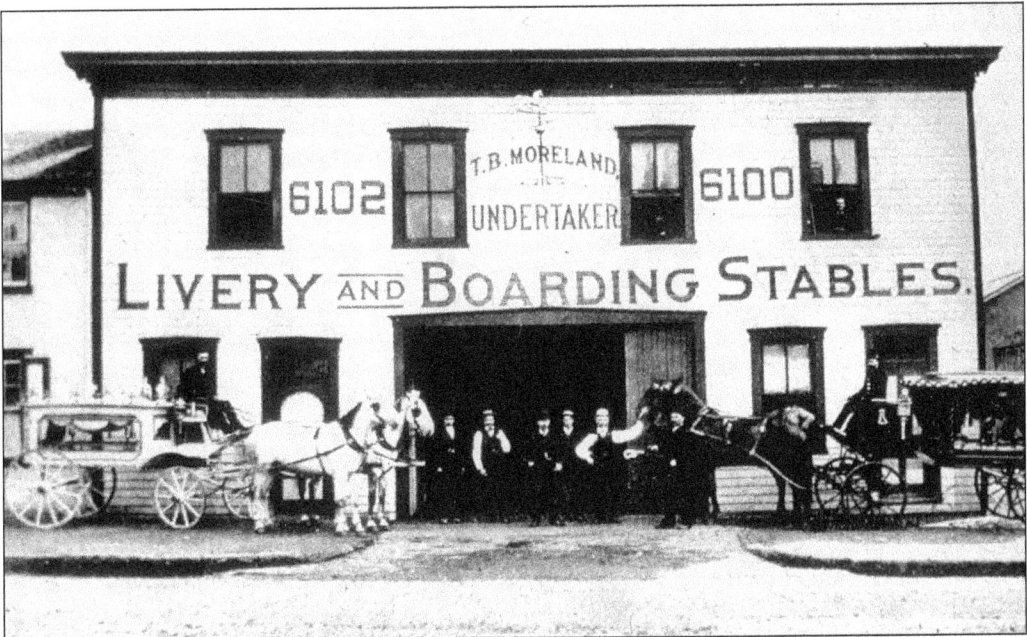

The exact location of this early commercial venture is unknown, but there was apparently no shortage of transportation to funerals with these enterprising gentlemen on call. Notice the horse-drawn hearses on either side.

Lyndhurst was the name of William Thaw's Gothic Revival home at 1165 Beechwood Boulevard. It was designed by architect Theophilus Parsons Chandler, and construction began in 1887. William Thaw's widow, Mary Thaw, later sold part of the property to raise funds for her son Harry's legal defense. Harry K. Thaw was arrested for murdering prominent architect Stanford White in 1906. Lyndhurst was demolished *c.* 1942.

Highmont was one of the mansions on Millionaires' Row in Pittsburgh. It stood at 6200 Fifth Avenue on the corner of Shady Avenue. The Chateauesque structure was built in 1888 for J. J. Vandergrift. Charles M. Schwab bought the house in 1900, and in 1903, he sold Highmont to Daniel M. Clemson, vice president of the Carnegie Steel Corporation. The building was torn down sometime before the 1950s.

These early Squirrel Hill commuters are presumably on their way to work. The horse-drawn carriage is a precursor to the modern-day bus, albeit a draftier one.

This is a small construction crew from the W. J. Hasley Company in 1904. The crew is seen working on the expansion of the Homewood Cemetery. The cemetery, incorporated in 1876, was situated on land previously belonging to the Honorable William Wilkins, a former U.S. senator and secretary of war. You can see some of the large mausoleums on the hillside above, along with headstones to the left of the work crew.

The home of Augustus A. Frauenheim is pictured here in 1905. Built at the turn of the century, it contained quite a few rooms, including a formal ballroom for large parties. The style is somewhat eclectic, containing elements of both Gothic and Queen Anne design. The Frauenheim house stood at the southwest corner of Beacon and Murdoch Streets and was torn down sometime prior to 1923.

Ben Elm is shown here in 1905. The Arts and Crafts–style home was designed by Frederick Law Olmsted Jr. for William Larimer Mellon, the president of the Gulf Oil Corporation. The building, which was demolished in 1951, was located at 5360 Forbes Avenue at the Darlington Road intersection.

This view, looking east on Forbes Avenue at the Darlington Road intersection, features two large houses at the entrance to Schenley Park. The house on the right is Ben Elm, the home of William Larimer Mellon.

Serpentine Drive, connecting Beacon Street to Darlington Road, is one of the roads going through Schenley Park. This postcard from 1906 includes the A. A. Frauenheim house (at Beacon and Murdoch) in the background on the left.

This view from April 19, 1909, shows a horse-drawn wagon near the intersection of Forward and Greenfield Avenues. The Squirrel Hill Tunnel was later constructed through the large hill in the background.

The John Worthington mansion, at 5505 Forbes Avenue, is shown prior to its acquisition by the congregation of Temple Sinai in 1946. Pittsburgh native Louis Stevens designed the Tudor-styled house in 1909.

This is one of the formal interior rooms of the John Worthington house. The cloisonne vase on the mantel and the molded-oak wall paneling indicate the wealth of John Worthington, who served as the director of the Union National Bank and was a former oil company director.

This view shows the library of the Worthington mansion. The plasterwork relief on the ceiling is particularly interesting. Some of the original features of the mansion were removed during its transition from private home to house of worship, but the beautiful gardens on the Murdoch Street side of the building have been restored to their former glory.

R. B. Melon, Residence,
. Ave. and Beechwood Boulevard,
   Pittsburgh, Pa.

The home of Richard Beatty Mellon, at 6500 Fifth Avenue, is shown in this c. 1915 postcard. The house stood at the corner of Fifth Avenue and Beechwood Boulevard. The Tudor-style house was built between 1907 and 1909 by the firm of Alden and Harlow, the same architects who designed many buildings in Pittsburgh, including the Carnegie Museum complex, the Duquesne Club, and Highmont.

Visitors to the Richard Beatty Mellon house would discharge their passengers under the porte-cochere to the left. Notice the attractive bay windows and the castellated tower.

The upstairs hall of the Richard Beatty Mellon house is featured here in beautiful detail. Notice the elaborately coffered ceiling, the Corinthian pilasters, and the delicate leaf design in the metal balustrade. The Mellon house contained 65 rooms, and there were formal gardens on the property. In 1941, the house was demolished. The land today is a part of Mellon Park. The old iron gates from the Mellon estate still enclose Mellon Park and the Pittsburgh Center for the Arts.

The gatehouse of the Homewood Cemetery is pictured in 1931. Note the ironwork on the gates, which were designed by Philadelphia artist Samuel Yellin. The Tudor Gothic–styled building was constructed in the late 1880s and was the original entrance to the cemetery on Dallas Avenue, at the Aylesboro Avenue intersection.

One of the more interesting areas within the Homewood Cemetery is Section 12, Lot 26, shown here in the mid-1920s. This small area contains the bodies of members of the Grand Army of the Republic, a group originally formed by soldiers and sailors who returned from the Civil War. Note the Civil War cannons with chains between them, marking the boundaries of the section.

The pyramid in the center is the Brown family mausoleum, in Section 14, Lot 40, of the Homewood Cemetery. It was built between 1905 and 1907 by W. Harry Brown, a wealthy coal baron. Brown owned an elaborate 50-room stone mansion on Fifth Avenue and traveled to Egypt and the Panama Canal. He passed away in 1921. The pyramid, originally designed by Alden and Harlow, has undergone numerous modifications since its original construction.

The landscape design of the Homewood Cemetery is the first example of the Lawn Park style in western Pennsylvania. This style, which became popular in the 19th century, employed minimal planting so that the landscape would appear natural and understated. Some of the design elements at the cemetery included a lily pond, a reflecting pool, and other parklike amenities. The lily pond is shown here c. 1923.

The intersection of Fifth and Shady Avenues is pictured in 1933. The large house to the left is the Charles D. Marshall home, at 6300 Fifth Avenue. The Georgian-style house was built between 1911 and 1912 by Charles Barton Keen. In 1945, it was donated to the City of Pittsburgh and leased by the Pittsburgh Center for the Arts. It is used as gallery space for artists, administrative offices, and a gift shop.

Andrew W. Mellon Hall is located on Woodland Road on the campus of Chatham College. From 1917 to 1940, it served as the home of Andrew W. Mellon, a prominent Pittsburgh banker and secretary of the Treasury. The Tudor Revival home was built for George M. Laughlin Jr. in 1902. Mellon enlarged the house and added tennis courts, bowling alleys, and an underground swimming pool. In 1940, his son Paul donated the house to Chatham College.

Three

COMMUNITY LIFE
AND CHURCHES

The early settlers in this area were religious people. They were not all of one denomination and did not always agree, but they respected each other and got along well. Sunday school for adults and children often formed the beginning of a church.

Three of the earliest churches in the area still have an active membership. The Mary S. Brown Memorial Methodist Episcopal Church (on Beechwood Boulevard near Forward Avenue) had as its predecessor the 1843 Brick Church, which was nearby. The Sixth Presbyterian Church's local predecessor was Mount of Olives Church (built in 1863), which stood where the current Colfax School is located. The Episcopal Church of the Redeemer, at 5700 Forbes Avenue, was first a temporary chapel at Woodmont and Wightman Streets in 1903.

There have been numerous religious groups in Squirrel Hill over the years. In 1941, the *Squirrel Hill News* listed nine worship sites: Asbury Methodist Church, Beechwood Chapel in the Roosevelt Annex School, Beth Shalom Congregation, Central Christian Church, Christian Science, Mary S. Brown Memorial Methodist Episcopal Church, Poale Zedeck Congregation, Sixth Presbyterian Church, and the Third United Presbyterian Church. The churches followed their congregations as they relocated from downtown to the Lower Hill to Oakland, Shadyside, or Squirrel Hill. Change continues today.

See chapter 8 for additional detail on the Squirrel Hill Jewish community.

The Mary S. Brown Memorial Methodist Episcopal Church began with John Turner's gift of land to the community. In 1843, a small brick church was built where the present parsonage stands. At one time, three denominations held services on alternate Sundays—Methodists, Presbyterians, and Baptists. Brown's Chapel (a larger, frame structure) was built in 1881 on the same location.

Disagreements occurred, attendance diminished, and no repairs were made. In 1892, the church was sold to W. A. Starr for $40. He tore it down and used the lumber to build two homes. In 1904, a temporary structure measuring 36 by 60 feet was put up on the old site until a new church building could be erected in memory of Mary Smith Brown, financed by her son.

Mary Smith Brown, a local settler, was the mother of Samuel Smith Brown, whose wealth came from coal transportation. The church and Brown's Hill Road are part of their legacy. Fifty feet of land adjoining the Turner Cemetery was purchased so the new church would front on Beechwood Boulevard. The cornerstone laid in 1908 contains a stone from the church of 1843. This photograph was taken in the 1920s.

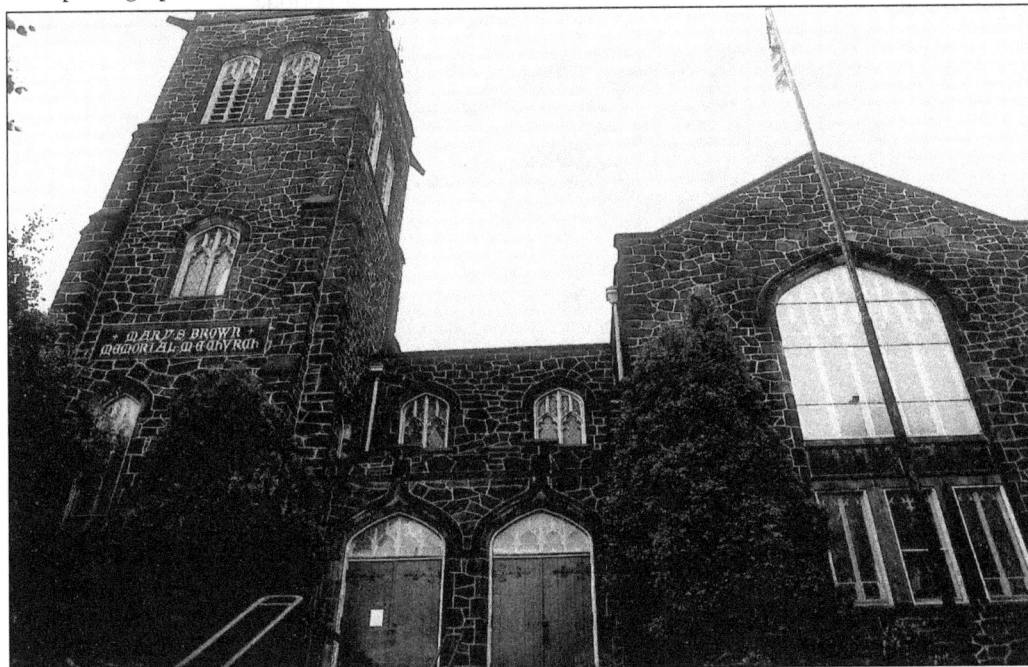

In 1941, the church (at that time 96 years old) united with the local Methodist Protestant congregation after a merger of their national churches. The Squirrel Hill Methodist Protestant Church, built in 1909 at the corner of Beechwood Boulevard and Lilac Street, was sold to the Church of the Brethren in 1942. Today Mary S. Brown Memorial Methodist Episcopal Church has a small involved membership.

Mount of Olives (later Mount Olivet) Presbyterian Church was organized in 1863. It was a viable institution until it closed in 1893. This photograph from 1908 shows the church's location on Phillips Avenue at Beechwood Boulevard. The church's neighbor, Colfax Public School, was rebuilt and expanded in 1911. The land where the church stood was taken over for the expansion, and the church was probably dismantled in that period.

The original Sixth Presbyterian Church began in 1836 with the Fort Pitt Sunday School, which met in the glass house (factory) of Curling and Robinson, at the corner of Washington and Franklin Streets. It organized as a church in 1850 and erected a new building (shown here) at the corner of Franklin and Townsend Streets (Lower Hill) in 1851–1852. Its parishioners began to move, and change was needed.

To meet the need of the Presbyterian congregation, a cornerstone was laid at Forbes and Murray Avenues for the present Sixth Presbyterian Church, on July 10, 1902. When the new building opened in 1903, it absorbed the former congregation of the nearby Mount Olivet Presbyterian Church. This is a view of citizens gathering around the Sixth Presbyterian Church on Armistice Day, November 11, 1918, the official end of World War I. Armistice Day became an annual day set aside to honor veterans of World War I.

In 1916, the Sixth Presbyterian Church congregation numbered 650, and the Sunday school had 450 members. Rev. Dr. J. Shane Nicholls presided as pastor from 1894 until 1919, when Rev. B. F. Farber took over. These photographs of Sunday school children were probably taken between 1910 and 1920.

The Sixth Presbyterian Church congregation peaked at about 1,000 members. During the 1960s, it was open to the dissenting voices being heard in religious organizations. It had a "coffeehouse" setting for its young people. "Happenings" and "be-ins" by nonmembers took place on its centrally located, massive steps. The congregation, then about 300 people, rethought its mission and focused as an inclusive Presbyterian congregation.

By the 1960s, the Sixth Presbyterian congregation was smaller. Its real estate became more valuable. There were years of controversy during the 1970s over development plans for the location. Opportunity and community approval eventually merged. The final settlement gave the congregation an endowment and funds to clean the stonework. The parking lot and village garden were replaced by an appropriate, contemporary residential building. This photograph was taken shortly before cleaning of the exterior. Today the Sixth Presbyterian Church offers its facilities for use by a variety of community groups, including the Squirrel Hill Historical Society.

From 1906 until 1966, the Asbury Methodist Church stood at the corner of Forbes and Murray Avenues, the site of the current Carnegie Library. This glimpse of the church tower (right) hints at the Gothic architecture of the stone edifice. The design, by O. M. Topp, was described as one of the most beautiful in the city. The building had a 500-person auditorium finished in mahogany with open timber trusses. This view up Murray Avenue from Bartlett Street dates from 1927.

In this view, only the front steps of the Asbury Methodist Church are visible along Forbes Avenue. The congregation originated in 1833 as a Sunday school downtown and then moved to the Lower Hill. Construction here began in 1906. The church was complete with Sunday school rooms, a library, a parlor for women, a gymnasium, and social rooms. By 1966, attendance declined. The church closed, and the congregation merged with the First Methodist Church in Shadyside.

In September 1900, Mrs. Charles P. Smith opened a Sunday school for her three children at her home at 1401 Wightman Street. Neighborhood children joined. By 1903, a group of energetic families organized a parish, set up a building fund, bought land at 5700 Forbes Avenue, and erected this temporary wooden chapel at Woodmont and Wightman Streets. It was the first Episcopal diocesan church to have a Young People's Society.

The permanent building for the congregation, the Church of the Redeemer was completed on its present site by 1913. In the early 1950s, space was made for a small school that soon became St. Edmund's Academy, which is today located next to the church. Flexible and open to diversity, Redeemer served as an early home for the Temple Sinai Jewish Reform congregation after it incorporated in 1946 but before it acquired the Worthington mansion to use as a sanctuary. Temple Sinai members met in the parish hall.

The Church of the Redeemer renovation began in 1936. The changes included rotating the church 90 degrees, setting it on new foundations, encasing it in Gothic limestone, and adding a stone bell tower. Designed by Lamont Button, the stone rectory (on Darlington Road) was erected in 1938. In 1939, the resplendent stained-glass church windows were begun. The windows were a labor of love by Howard Gilmann Wilbert, who designed and executed them, completing the project in 1962. This a present-day view of the church.

St. Philomena (founded by the Redemptorists Order) originated in 1839 as a Catholic church in the Strip district. By 1917, the congregation moved out of the increasingly industrial downtown. The Redemptorists relocated to Squirrel Hill on seven acres bounded by Forward Avenue and Beechwood Boulevard. Work began on a Catholic school that would include a church. The new school was ready in 1922. The building was designed by architect John T. Comes.

In 1928, work began on an extension of the St. Philomena church-school building. Two additional stories were added. Church facilities were renovated. The parish served the community for over 60 years, but the congregation began moving away again. The final mass was celebrated on June 27, 1993. The building was later sold to Community Day to be used as a school.

Four

EARLY SCHOOLS

The history of local schools is not well documented until Liberty Township (which included Squirrel Hill) became part of Pittsburgh in 1867.

Pioneers wanted an education for their children. One of the earliest schools employed James Fleming as its first teacher; he was the son of the James Fleming who came to Pittsburgh in 1759 and settled here later. David Irwin Jr., another pioneer's son, became the second teacher. Quite probably, the first classes took place before there was a school building.

The first known school building was a log cabin specifically built as a school on land owned by the Fleming family (near what is now Phillips Avenue and Frick Park). Around 1840, James Fleming, the teacher, built a small brick school on Forbes Avenue between Shady and Murray Avenues.

John Turner gave the community a quarter acre of land for a school in 1836. On it was eventually located the first Free School. It was a predecessor of the Squirrel Hill School, which was located on Bigelow Street between McCaslin Street and Hazelwood Avenue.

Early schools, as traced in photographs, are Forward Avenue School, Colfax, Roosevelt School, and Wightman. The Roosevelt School seen on page 48 was the second with this name. Originally at Saline Street and Beechwood Boulevard, it opened in 1885 and was replaced by the new school. When Roosevelt became crowded, it was reopened as the Roosevelt Annex. It closed in the 1930s and was sold in 1941 to the Christian Assembly (Plymouth Brethren).

Swisshelm and Brown Schools were part of Liberty Township School before the merger with the city. These schools today would be considered outside of Squirrel Hill boundaries. Today, as yesterday, schools open, close, find reuse, or are torn down depending on money, population shifts, and whether larger, newer schools absorbed student groups.

Squirrel Hill is bordered today by Carnegie Mellon University and the adjacent University of Pittsburgh. Chatham College, however, is the institution of higher education that is most a part of Squirrel Hill's early history and has been featured in this chapter. The school was organized as Pennsylvania Female College (1869–1890), was renamed the Pennsylvania College for Women (1890–1955), and most recently became Chatham College. Over time, the college has acquired some of the fine homes that surrounded it when it began and has adaptively reused them as part of the campus.

The Forward Avenue School was built in 1886 at Artisan Street and was razed in 1923. This property was sold to the State of Pennsylvania in 1952 for the development of the Parkway East. An earlier school (Liberty Township School) was also on Forward Avenue but was located below where Taylor Allderdice High School is now. This earlier school operated for five years and then became a private home again.

When Squirrel Hill became part of Pittsburgh, the next school built here was also on Forward Avenue. In its first year, the original one-room schoolhouse had 115 students, one principal, and one teacher. Five years later (in 1873), this larger frame schoolhouse (Colfax No. 1) on Phillips Avenue opened to 324 students, one principal, and four teachers. It offered no inside plumbing. This photograph is from the 1880s.

Beechwood Boulevard was just a farm road. Teachers used the electric trolley line that came on Murray Avenue. There was a dangerous marshy spot at the intersection of Phillips and Shady Avenues, where quicksand had taken some lives. The teachers also avoided going by way of Munhall-Hobart or Beacon (then paths), for the area contained abandoned coal mines and was inhabited by unsavory characters.

Some teachers preferred to get off the trolley car at Forbes and Shady Avenues. They would put cleats on their overshoes, climb over fences, and hike through farmlands and orchards. Beechwood Boulevard was cut through from Aylesboro in 1898. The present Colfax School, at 2332 Beechwood, was built in 1911. It was named after Schuyler Colfax, vice president during Pres. Ulysses S. Grant's first term.

The second Roosevelt School (upper left) is pictured in 1913. At this time, an electric trolley line is being built along Murray Avenue between Loretta and Lilac Streets. Named after Theodore Roosevelt, the school opened in 1908. In 1955, a replacement school was built on Lilac Street between Shady Avenue and Saline Street. It was eventually named the John Minadeo School.

The Sterrett Sub-District School (in Squirrel Hill), later replaced by the Linden School (outside of Squirrel Hill), was first built because small children had too difficult a time walking to the widely separated Colfax District schools. It was a one-story building built in 1892 on Linden Avenue near Edgerton. It was part of the district that had been subdivided from the Colfax District in 1877. This photograph of Reynolds Street at Linden Avenue dates from 1913.

In 1898, the Thomas Wightman School opened in the Colfax District on Solway Street between Wightman and Negley Avenues. The building was expanded in 1904 and closed in 1980. It was bought by the Squirrel Hill Urban Coalition, which later sold it to the Carriage House Children's Center. This photograph is from the 1920s.

Designed by architect Ulysses J. L. Peoples, the original Wightman School building contained five classrooms. The same firm enlarged it to include 13 rooms, a library, and a third-floor gymnasium. The Romanesque style of the new wing was decorated with ornate cherubic friezes, intricate stained-glass windows, and an elaborate façade on the stage. This photograph may show a May Day event.

The rolling hills between Wilkins and Fifth Avenues were settled around the time of the Civil War by a small group of interrelated influential families who built one of Pittsburgh's grandest housing developments. Seen in the early 1860s is the George A. Berry house. In 1869, Berry sold the house and grounds to the founders of the Pennsylvania Female College (Chatham College).

The college's entire student body is shown in front of Berry Hall in 1885. Demolished in 1952, the building was said to be the largest private residence in Allegheny County when it was built. Initially, everything took place in Berry—all classes, dining, and boarding for students, faculty, and administration. Dilworth Hall, an addition, was built in 1889. Today, 406 students live on campus, and 1,250 attend classes.

This c. 1880s Latin class was taught by Mary Pike. On Woodland Road from Wilkins, the college now owns five mansions on one side (from Berry House to Fickes House). On the other side, it owns Gregg House and Mellon Center (the biggest on the road). Across the stone bridge, the college owns Spencer House. At the Fifth Avenue entrance stands the restored Howe-Childs Gate House.

Shown is the Pennsylvania Female College (Chatham College) class of 1888. From left to right are the following: (first row) Martha Lockhart, Dorcas Beer, and Elizabeth Simpson; (second row) Elizabeth Boale, Hetty Boyle, Elizabeth Kirk, and Alice Stockton.

Students are shown on the porch of Berry Hall, at the Pennsylvania College for Women (Chatham College), in 1893.

The 1902 senior class of the Pennsylvania College for Women (Chatham College) is shown on the steps of Berry Hall.

Students are seen outside Dilworth Hall c. 1907. To the right is a Tiffany window installed in 1889. The newly formed alumnae association raised funds to commemorate the classes of 1873 to 1888. They commissioned little-known glassmaker Louis Comfort Tiffany to make a chapel window. The window has been restored and now hangs in the Buhl Hall Science Laboratory Building.

These c. 1905 commencement exercises were held in the chapel of Dilworth Hall. Note the stained-glass window in the background. The Tiffany window is out of frame to the left.

This photograph was taken on May Day 1909 in front of Berry Hall. The college's May Day festivals were so popular that they were said to draw crowds in the thousands.

On May 2, 1910, Pres. William Taft (the rotund man in the dark coat) greets students and alumnae of the college. They are on the porch of present-day Andrew W. Mellon Hall. The uniformed figure on the left is Archibald Butt, the president's personal aid. Standing next to Taft, one step above, is college president Henry Lindsay.

Five

SCHENLEY PARK

Squirrel Hill is surrounded by Schenley, Frick, and Mellon Parks, which provide natural enjoyment, recreation, and a respite from cityscapes. Each park is just minutes from any Squirrel Hill home. Schenley Park is the oldest of the three parks, the second largest, and the most utilized. It serves as a tranquil transition from the bustling and monumental character of Oakland's many public and educational institutions.

Most of the land that was to become the park was acquired by Gen. James O'Hara. His granddaughter Mary Croghan Schenley inherited this land, but not without scandal and legalities. In 1842, Mary eloped to England at a tender age (14 or 15) to marry Capt. Edward W. H. Schenley, thus creating an international scandal. Mary's later claim for her inheritance prevailed in court. In 1889, the land (called Mount Airy) was being considered for a housing development. While Mary had never returned to Pittsburgh, an appeal to her led to her donation of 300 acres of land to the city. She optioned 120 additional acres for purchase with the stipulation that the land be called Schenley Park and that it could never be sold or privately developed. The city quickly bought the 120 acres for $100,000, and over time, other tracts were donated or purchased to bring the park's total to 455 acres.

Edward Manning Bigelow was Pittsburgh's city engineer. In 1889, he was appointed director of the department of public works. Bigelow had a vision for Pittsburgh's park system and was behind the quest for land. Through his efforts, British landscape architect William Falconer was hired as superintendent of Schenley Park in 1896. In a few short years, Schenley Park's quintessential design was in place.

The intense work at the turn of the century was well appreciated as people flocked to the park. It was exciting and entertaining. Attractions included bridle paths, walking trails, a lake, a racetrack, a lily pond, a picnic area, a band shell, a golf course, a boathouse, and a carousel. Today some of these features remain and are in use. An electrified fountain with dancing waters at the base of Flagstaff Hill did not last. The first zoo and aquarium for the city were moved to Highland Park in 1898. Some other attractions were removed or were replaced by newer features, such as playgrounds.

Over the years, the maintenance of the city parks has fallen behind. However, with the work of the Pittsburgh Parks Conservancy, the parks are regaining their luster. This chapter offers a glimpse of Schenley Park's early days.

THE O'HARA HOMESTEAD,
BIRTHPLACE OF MRS. MARY E. SCHENLEY.

James O'Hara was an early settler, a pioneer in the glassmaking business, and also the first U.S. quartermaster general. He had the foresight to purchase large tracts of land throughout the area, including the land that became Schenley Park.

This *c.* 1909 photograph shows the newly built Forbes Field baseball stadium (right). The garden walk that replaced the Casino (which operated between 1894 and 1896) is in the middle background. The Carnegie Museum (before the sycamore trees and plaza) faces the St. Pierre Ravine and Bellefield Bridge. In 1915, the ravine was filled in. The Junction Hollow and Panther Hollow bridges are complete, Phipps Conservatory (back right) is visible, and the racetrack grandstand is on the horizon.

Edward Bigelow's original plans for a park fit well with the structures in Oakland that were soon around it. Phipps Conservatory (1893), the Carnegie Music Hall and Museum (1895), and the Casino (shown here) were at its entrance. They were very popular.

The Casino, a grand ice-skating and dance pavilion, opened in 1894. It was in use for only 18 months before it was destroyed by fire. After that, the site was a formal flower garden. In the 1960s, the city allowed Helen Clay Frick to use the site for the construction of the Frick Fine Arts Building of the University of Pittsburgh.

Phipps Conservatory was the second and biggest conservatory that Henry Phipps gifted to the city. Phipps's fortune came from real estate and steel. The conservatory was designed and built by the noted New York greenhouse firm Lord and Burnham of Irvington-on-the-Hudson. Their spectacular creation featured nine display houses with "silvered" domes and glass vaults. It opened with a large collection of tropical plants from the Colombian Exposition in Chicago. From 1893 on, Phipps Conservatory was a major attraction in new Schenley Park. An estimated 350,000 people visited Phipps Conservatory in 1894. The conservatory was operated for 100 years by the city. In 1993, Phipps Conservatory signed a 100-year lease to manage the facility for the city.

A nursery was created in Schenley Park to supply plants and trees for all of Pittsburgh's parks. In 1896, some 20,000 perennial flowers were planted in Schenley Park's ravines. Trees went in. Planted by the row and the grove, they included pin oaks, plane trees, Norway and silver maples, fast-growing catalpas, buckeyes, and American elms. Year after year, similar effort was poured into the parks. The ginkgo trees along Schenley Drive were planted in 1906.

Paths were constructed. A picnic area was erected in Panther Hollow in 1892. An existing quarry in the park provided stone for many drives and walks. In 1891, a 250-foot-long stone wall was built on the main road with that stone. The wall at Serpentine Drive was completed with 2,467 feet of handsome coping and finished with four stone pillars. This path is in Panther Hollow near the lake.

59

Even before the lake in the park was formally completed, it was a natural attraction. Here, a Sunday afternoon finds strollers on Panther Hollow Bridge, overlooking recreational activity around the lake.

In 1902, some 70,000 locust trees were listed as planted on the bare slopes of Junction Hollow. (Records are not clear as to whether this is a cumulative figure or the total for the year.)

Lily Pond, in Schenley Park, was designed by parks superintendent William Falconer in 1897. It reflects the naturalistically designed landscapes of the 19th century. The George Westinghouse Memorial Pond replaced it in 1930.

This tufa-stone bridge (one of two in the Panther Hollow area) was built in 1908. The bridle paths were also popular with bicyclists. In 1897, sixteen rustic bridges were constructed over the streamlets in the ravines of the park. Only traces are left today. Additional entrances, such as the Murdoch and Beacon entrances, were built and macadamized.

A golf club was created in 1896 by a group of leading East End business and professional leaders. The course was on the lands of Schenley Park. A year later, the Pittsburgh Golf Club had a new clubhouse designed by Alden and Harlow on land just outside the park. The city and the club did not see eye to eye over the club having exclusive rights over public land.

By 1910, it was decided that the city open the Schenley Park Golf Links to the public and build its own clubhouse a few hundred yards away. The members found other space for private golf but have remained in their building to this day. In 1912, Pittsburgh mayor William Magee officially opened this city golf shelter, equipped with lockers, showers, lounges, and a veranda, still in use.

Henry Clay Frick, a Pittsburgh Golf Club member, had numerous tracts of land in the East End. A piece of his holdings was used for the private Country Club of Allegheny County. It was near Beechwood Boulevard and Phillips Avenue, with entrances off Douglas Avenue. In this photograph, the W. J. Hasley Company is building the country club using a steam shovel. The club operated for a number of years and became part of Frick Park in 1935.

A music pavilion was erected in Schenley Park in 1898. It was designed by Rutan and Russell. Costing $7,000, it measured 73 feet in length, 32 feet in width, and 45 feet in height. It was lighted by 180 incandescent lights. The band shell remained until the late 1930s. The Anderson playground is on the spot now.

Shelter House and Speedway, Schenley Park,
Pittsburgh, Pa.

The Schenley Park Visitor Center, the only remaining original park building, stands adjacent to Phipps Conservatory near the Panther Hollow Bridge. The center started life between 1904 and 1911 as a picnic shelter designed in the Arts and Craft style by Pittsburgh architectural firm Rutan and Russell. It served variously as a nature museum, concession stand, garden club center, and tool shed. The restoration was completed in 2001.

The Panther Hollow Bridge, constructed in 1897, is seen here c. 1910. It is a steel-and-stone bridge constructed by the Schutz, Hridsge and Iron Company. Each corner is ornamented by a panther designed in bronze by Guiseppe Moretti. The panthers measure four feet six inches by six feet four inches. On the horizon is the racetrack grandstand that was on Schenley Oval.

In 1893, a half-mile, kite-shaped racetrack was constructed in Schenley Park. It was used for horse racing and was called a speedway. In 1907, the grandstands shown here were completed and became very popular.

In 1911, stables were added. Frequent fires were a serious problem and left the grandstand in poor condition. In 1914, it was scheduled to be razed. Other Schenley Park recreational facilities included three baseball grounds completed in 1907. In 1913–1914, tennis courts were constructed. Track-and-field activities also expanded.

Carousels were planned for several city parks. The merry-go-rounds were 50 feet in diameter and had 46 artistically carved life-size animals and four double-seated chariots. Schenley's opened in 1913. It was located at the top of Panther Hollow and the corner of Panther Hollow Drive and Greenfield Road. The carousel ceased operation in 1940 and was later removed.

Bigelow Monument, Schenley Park, Pittsburgh, Pa.

The plaque on this monument to Edward Bigelow calls him the "Father of the City's Parks." It stands on Schenley Drive at Phipps Conservatory. The nine-foot-tall bronze designed by Guiseppe Moretti was the first piece of sculpture dedicated in Schenley Park. On the day it was dedicated, July 4, 1895, some 60,000 people were present. "The Bigelow March" was written for the event.

Panther Hollow Lake was gradually developed from a stream and small lake c. 1900. Informally known as Lake Bigelow and sometimes Lake Carnegie (another of this name was in Highland Park), it was used for boating in summer and skating in winter. This image shows the lake in its natural state, with small islands.

In 1909, Panther Hollow Lake was completed. It became a major attraction and favorite subject of photographers. The boathouse was added by 1911. It was damaged by fire and was torn down c. 1980.

This view from the 1920s shows Panther Hollow Lake in its prime. The scene is a far cry from Panther Hollow's beginnings as a barren, steep ravine crossed by railroad tracks and a quarry. The railroad tracks from Junction Hollow through Panther Hollow are still in use.

Plans are being proposed to restore Panther Hollow Lake to its former glory.

Six

SQUIRREL HILL
IN TRANSITION

Squirrel Hill had relatively few paved roads until after 1900. Furthermore, the neighborhood had limited road and public transportation links until the end of the 19th century. Indeed, some major highways into the area, such as the Boulevard of the Allies, were not constructed until the 1920s. In addition, many of the owners of the area's farms and estates were not yet ready to give up their "country living." As a result, it was not surprising that Squirrel Hill in 1900 remained substantially less built up than adjacent areas.

In chapter 2, we documented the transition of portions of Squirrel Hill from farms and undeveloped rural area into country estates owned by the wealthiest families in the Pittsburgh area. Between 1900 and 1920, a second transition took place, with Squirrel Hill changing from a residential and agricultural area into a more urban and built-up residential community. The profits available from residential subdivision became so great that the owners of both the older farms and the more recently developed estates began to sell their properties for smaller lot development.

There is little doubt that the 1893 construction of electric trolleys along Forbes and Murray Avenues, the design of Beechwood Boulevard by Frederick Law Olmsted Jr. (with construction in 1903), and the gradual paving of other Squirrel Hill roads were key factors in the buildup of the area.

We have been fortunate to have a large number of photographs of Squirrel Hill in transition from 1900 to 1920 and are pleased to include those views in this chapter. The older photographs show how much of the area was still rural at that time and how many streets were not yet paved. The later scenes include blocks that have already been predominantly (but not fully) developed into homes on smaller lots. Several of the photographs are of homes on Murray Hill Avenue, one of the neighborhood's first built-up areas and now Squirrel Hill's only designated historic district.

The first few pictures in this chapter represent the central portion of Squirrel Hill. This view, looking east, shows the intersection of Phillips and Murray Avenues in October 1908. Over the next decades, both streets became residential areas, but Murray Avenue later turned into a commercial area.

Phillips Avenue is seen in a photograph taken from Murray Avenue, looking east toward Shady Avenue. Residential development along Phillips has just begun, and the right-of-way has yet to be paved.

Seen here is another view of Phillips Avenue.

This October 1908 view, looking east, shows Phillips Avenue at the intersection with Shady Avenue. As in the previous photographs, residential subdivision of previous farms is just beginning.

Midway Street at Shady Avenue is pictured in a view looking west on October 21, 1908. A portion of Midway Street is now called Morrowfield Avenue, and the remainder appears to have been eliminated, probably due to construction of the Squirrel Hill Tunnel, which now runs under this location.

Midway Street at Murray Avenue is shown in a view looking east on October 21, 1908. This location is probably where the Morrowfield Hotel now stands. The tracks of the Pittsburgh Railways electric trolley can be seen along Murray Avenue. Trains that ran along this line over the years were No. 60, No. 68, and No. 80.

Forward Avenue is seen in a 1908 view looking east. Residential development is just under way. This residential area is now close to the new Summerset at Frick planned residential community.

The next group of photographs shows the northern portion of the neighborhood. This is a view of residential development at Fair Oaks Avenue between South Negley Avenue and Wilkins Avenue, on the north side of Squirrel Hill. This picture was taken in April 1909, prior to any cobblestone or other pavement.

The home at 1168 Murray Hill Avenue, one of Squirrel Hill's most historic streets, was designed in the Queen Anne style. Murray Hill Avenue, located near the Chatham College campus, is the neighborhood's only designated historic district. The Murray Hill District includes 40 homes constructed after 1890, sited on a particularly dramatic hillside street. Murray Hill's proximity to such city amenities as a streetcar line along Fifth Avenue combined with its bucolic residential design earned it the Latin nickname *Rus in Urbe* (a bit of country in the city). It includes a number of Queen Anne and Colonial Revival homes, augmented by an occasional Shingle-style dwelling.

Seen here is a present-day view of the home at 1160 Murray Hill Avenue. This residence was once the home of Judge Samuel A. McClung. The author Willa Cather lived in an attic apartment from 1896 to 1906 (during which time she taught at Central and Allegheny High Schools) and returned to live in the same residence between 1913 and 1915. During her time in Pittsburgh, Cather wrote *April Twilights* (1903), *Youth and the Bright Medusa* (1905), *O Pioneers* (1913), and *The Song of the Lark* (1915).

South Negley Avenue is seen in a photograph taken from Wilkins Avenue, looking toward Fair Oaks Avenue, in April 1909. Residential development is just getting under way.

The following pictures are all of the western portion of Forward Avenue, a road that runs along the south side of Squirrel Hill. A century ago, Forward Avenue also ran west into the adjacent area of Greenfield, but the construction of the Parkway East and the Squirrel Hill Tunnel in the 1950s eliminated this portion of Forward Avenue. This set of photographs provides a good view of early development at the edge of the neighborhood. This 1905 view, looking south, shows Forward Avenue below Lewis Street, within a block of the southern boundary of Schenley Park. Lewis Street was also eliminated by the parkway construction.

Forward Avenue is pictured in a view looking east from Boundary Street in 1908. This location is near the southwest boundary of Schenley Park.

Forward Avenue is shown at the Nixon Street intersection in a view looking south in November 1908. Nixon Street, which ran along the south boundary of Schenley Park, was later renamed Naylor Street. It was partially eliminated by Parkway East construction. A portion of Naylor Street now runs through Schenley Park. The western part of Saline Street is now located in this general area.

Forward Avenue at Nixon Street is pictured in a view looking south in November 1908. The railroad tracks in this and the previous picture are not one of the city's streetcar lines. They may be a spur line connecting to a Pennsylvania Railroad track that ran along the western boundary of Schenley Park. A portion of the latter line still runs through Oakland's Panther Hollow.

Forward Avenue at Alexis Street is pictured in September 1908. Alexis Street is south of Schenley Park at its western boundary and still exists.

Forward Avenue at Anthony Street is seen in a view looking south in November 1908. This area is two blocks from Forward Avenue and Alexis Street. Anthony Street no longer exists.

This view of Forward Avenue looks toward Sylvan Avenue in January 1910. The site is near the current right-of-way of Greenfield Avenue and the Monongahela River.

The next two pictures are from the central portion of Squirrel Hill, but at a somewhat later date. This is a view of Hobart Street and Wightman Street near Schenley Park in May 1913. Prior to 1910, Hobart Street was called Munhall Street west of Murray Avenue and also did not connect directly with Murray. There was limited residential development on this street at that time. The photograph shows a train along a railroad line that ran along Hobart at that time, probably for temporary construction purposes. The train appears to be dumping fill along the road side.

Hobart Street is seen in a May 1913 view looking east. When this photograph was taken, Hobart Street had been recently extended toward Murray Avenue. As a new right-of-way, the street has virtually no development.

The intersection of Murray and Flemington Avenues, south of central Squirrel Hill, is seen in a view looking south in May 1913. This photograph shows the Pittsburgh Railways electric trolley line.

Taken in May 1913 at the corner of Murray and Hazelwood Avenues, this photograph offers another view of the Pittsburgh Railways electric trolley line.

The current Linden School, near Beachwood Boulevard, was opened in 1903. The school replaced the Sterrett Sub-District School. Although Linden School is located in the adjacent Point Breeze area, photographs of the school have been included in this history because Linden School has always served numerous students from Squirrel Hill. The original structure was of the finest type of school construction, and Linden was one of few schools equipped with its own electricity-generating system. In 1918, Thomas L. Pfarr, the Allegheny County fire marshal, called Linden the safest school in the county. The original Linden School was expanded in 1922 and again in 1927–1928. This photograph was taken during the 1927–1928 expansion. Architect Thomas Pringle designed the addition.

Shown is another view of the 1927–1928 Linden School renovations. In 1903, Linden had a total enrollment of 170 pupils, increased to 730 by 1953. The original structure had eight rooms. More classrooms were created over the years by using hallway space and even temporary buildings. The school has frequently had overcrowding problems.

Linden School is shown in 1929, after renovation was completed. The school gained eight new classrooms in this expansion. The addition resulted from the effective leadership of Belle S. McMillen, who had been with the school since its early years and became principal in 1923. Additional impetus for the new construction came from the Linden Parent-Teacher Association, formed in 1925. The addition stopped plans to move Linden's seventh and eighth graders to the new Taylor Allderdice High School. Another addition to Linden School was built in 1960.

A horse-drawn buggy, the transportation of the early 20th century, travels along a paved road.

An early automobile with engine problems is being pushed to an unknown location.

Two horse-drawn buggies are being walked past an early automobile on a badly rutted dirt road.

An early car is shown in a farm area along a dirt road. Any doubt about the importance of paved roads for urban development is removed by these photographs.

Seven

RESIDENTIAL GROWTH AND FRICK PARK

The trend toward residential buildup documented in the previous chapter continued beyond 1920 and was predominantly completed during the 1930s. Of course, change is constant, and Squirrel Hill has continued to experience modifications in specific land uses to the present day. For example, Murray Avenue was first built up for residential use and then changed into a commercial corridor by the 1930s.

The first set of photographs included in this chapter features the residential areas that experienced development from 1920 to the early 1940s.

As Squirrel Hill became a built-up community with a larger population, additional schools were required. In this chapter, we have included photographs of Davis School and Taylor Allderdice High School, both of which were built in the late 1920s and early 1930s. Many of the photographs show the original construction of these two schools.

In chapter 5, we celebrated the history of Schenley Park. In 1927, Frick Park, Squirrel Hill's other great park, was opened thanks to the generosity of Henry Clay Frick. Frick Park is one of the crown jewels of the neighborhood, and we have featured it in this chapter.

South Negley Avenue is pictured from Wilkins Avenue in August 1924. Smaller homes have replaced the older farms, estates, and vacant land.

This view shows the intersection of Pocusset Street and Forward Avenue from Beechwood Boulevard in 1924.

Shown is another view looking toward Pocusset Street and Forward Avenue in 1924. The street is now built up with residential homes.

Pictured here is the Thaw House, on Beechwood Boulevard. Chapter 2 features a detailed background on the Thaw House.

Seen is the Scheibler House, at 2557 Beechwood Boulevard.

This view, looking down Forbes Avenue from the Murray Avenue intersection toward Schenley Park, shows central Squirrel Hill in 1927. On the right are the Forbes Terrace Townhouses, which were completely modernized in the late 1990s. The apartment houses on the left were demolished, and today this is the site of the Jewish Community Center. Farther down the block on the left is the Church of the Redeemer. In 1950, the St. Edmund's Academy was built next to this church.

Esther Tucker, a founding member of the Squirrel Hill Historical Society and contributor to this book, is shown standing in front of Forbes Terrace in 1941.

Mount Royal Road, opposite Fernwald Road, is shown in a view looking north in January 1928. At that time, this road had limited development and had not yet been paved.

Residences at Forward Avenue and Tilbury Street are shown in June 1935. These homes, across from Taylor Allderdice High School, are still occupied.

This view of Forward Avenue looks west toward Wightman Street. The portion of the street in this picture is now called Pocusset, and terrain in this area was changed substantially after construction of the Squirrel Hill Tunnel.

An electric trolley is shown on Forbes Avenue in a picture taken from Murray Avenue in 1932. The lines that ran on Forbes Avenue were Nos. 63–64, Nos. 66–69, and No. 80. Nos. 68 and 80 turned south onto Murray Avenue.

The intersection of Hazelwood and Murray Avenues is shown during in the 1930s or 1940s. A Pittsburgh Railways trolley car is going around a large curve in the tracks.

A peddler and wagon are shown on Hobart Street in July 1936.

Davis School, located on Phillips Avenue between Forbes Avenue and Wightman Street, was named for Dr. H. B. Davis, who was principal of the Henry Clay Frick Training School for Teachers. This picture shows the original construction of the school (1931–1932), as well as the recently completed Taylor Allderdice High School in the background.

This photograph shows interior construction of Davis School in January 1932. At the time of construction, it was expected that this school would eventually be expanded to include a second wing, a second story on each wing, and construction of a connecting central unit. However, since the vicinity of the school was soon built up with apartment houses with few school-age children, there was not enough demand to justify expansion for nearly 25 years. Nonetheless, with only four original classrooms and a kindergarten, the school frequently had to promote its pupils to either Wightman School or Colfax School due to overcrowding. Between 1940 and 1955, Davis School often had students only up to the second grade.

Construction of the Davis School boiler room is in progress in 1932. The school was expanded in 1955. The architect was Francis W. Swein. The new addition included two classrooms, a playroom, a doctor's office, a teachers' room, and an administrative office. The expansion allowed the school to retain children through the third grade. By 1957–1958, Davis School had an enrollment of 250. By 1980, however, changing demographics led to the closing of the school.

This photograph shows exterior construction of the Taylor Allderdice High School in July 1926. The architect for the new facility was Robert Maurice Trimble. The school was named to honor a former member of the Pittsburgh Board of Education and (earlier) the local board of the Colfax District.

Taylor Allderdice had his first job as a messenger, earning $4 per week. He started his industrial career as a mill worker at the age of 18. He left work to get a college education but soon returned to industry, eventually managing the largest tube company in the world. By the late 1920s, Allderdice had become president of the National Tube Company. This photograph from 1928 shows the construction of the auditorium for the new school.

When the Pittsburgh school code of 1911 was adopted, Allderdice was appointed one of the charter members of the new school board. He stayed interested in education for the remainder of his life, serving as vice chairman and chairman of the building and supply committee for many years. This photograph shows construction of the Taylor Allderdice School pool in 1928.

Taylor Allderdice High School was initially completed in 1927–1928, with 207,000 square feet of floor space. Key exterior features of the original construction included six guardian Ionic columns and a long green terrace. The school attendance quickly outgrew the space, and by 1930, a new addition (pictured here) was under construction at the rear of the original structure.

©PHOTO BY V. L. HUBBARD

61389

Generally considered to be of Georgian design, Taylor Allderdice occupies a full city block. It is elevated at the front, looking down on adjacent residences on Shady and Forward Avenues.

656   JUN 9 - 1937   TAYLOR ALLDERDICE HIGH SCHOOL, SQUIRREL HILL, PITTSBURGH, PA.

6A-H2142

Important changes that have been made in Taylor Allderdice since its construction include the completion of new chemistry and physics laboratories. By 1935, enrollment in the school was 3,400.

Mark Iskowitz, contributor to this book, is on the way to school in the late 1950s. Schools within walking distance were important for the residential attractiveness of Squirrel Hill.

As shown in this August 1926 photograph, an annual swim meet was held at the Schenley Park swimming pool. The pool, Pittsburgh's first public facility of its kind, was constructed in 1921. It was replaced with a larger pool in 1937.

Here is another view of the 1926 swim meet.

This photograph of the tourist camp in Schenley Park was taken in 1926. No detailed history is available of this camp, but based on the vehicles in this and the next photograph, visitors to the camp appear to have been well-off.

This is another view of the Schenley Park tourist camp.

In 1908, Henry Clay Frick told his 17-year-old daughter, Helen Frick, that she could have anything she wanted for her debutant party. She asked for a park where the children of Pittsburgh could enjoy nature, and her wish came true. When Frick died in 1919, he bequeathed 150 acres south of his Point Breeze mansion, Clayton, for a new park and provided a $2 million trust fund to help with maintenance of the park. The donated site was called the Gunn Hill tract after one of its early owners. Frick Park is shown shortly after it opened in 1927.

Seen here is one of Frick Park's many landscaped meadows. The original master plan for Frick Park (February 1927) was prepared by the firm of Lowell and Vinal, who had been retained by the executors of Henry Clay Frick's will. However, Mr. Lowell died just before the opening of Frick Park, and responsibility for the planning and design of the park was transferred to the Pittsburgh firm of Blum, Weldin and Company, mining and civil engineers with limited experience in park design.

From 1919 to 1942, the Frick Park trustees acquired 306.5 acres of additional park property in 39 purchases involving an expenditure of $899,065. Probably the most significant addition (1936) was the old Pittsburgh Country Club property (90 acres). Over the years, Frick Park grew to nearly 500 areas, the largest park in the area. This photograph shows Frick Park at English Lane.

During 1931–1935, the Frick family engaged famed architect John Russell Pope to design three Frick Park entrances. This commission reportedly took place while Pope was planning and supervising the conversion of the Frick Mansion in New York City into a museum. The three entrances were constructed with $70,000 in funds provided by the U.S. Works Progress Administration (WPA). This photograph is a view of the stone entrance to the park at Beechwood Boulevard.

This view from Frick Park toward Beechwood Boulevard shows the Pope gatehouses in the background and lines of sycamore trees on both sides of the road. In January 1935, the Frick executors retailed the Roslyn, New York, firm of Innnocenti and Webel, one of the most prestigious landmark architectural firms in the nation, to design Frick Park. In 1940, a 20-acre lawn (included in this photograph) was graded, topsoiled, fertilized, and seeded around the gatehouses. The landscaping project also included 21 large trees that were shifted from the country club.

This February 1937 view shows the entry greens and flagstone paving at the Beechwood Boulevard entrance, with the Pope gatehouses to each side out of view. The fountain pool was reportedly constructed at about this time.

Shown is another view of Beechwood Boulevard at Frick Park. This area is layered with history. Part of Nemacolin's Trail (Braddock's Road) once passed through here. The pioneer farm of James Fleming and his descendants and the Phillip and English Farms were here. Later the tennis courts of the Pittsburgh Country Club were nearby. Now the Blue Slide Playground attracts people.

This view shows the Reynolds Avenue entrance to Frick Park. The view is within a block of Clayton, the Frick estate in Pittsburgh. Clayton has now been opened to the public as the Frick Art and History Center, one of Pittsburgh's premier visitor attractions.

This a view of Pope's Frick Park Reynolds Avenue gatehouse, located just beyond the view pictured in the previous photograph.

103

This view of Frick Park shows the Braddock Avenue side of the park. To the left is the valley leading to Nine Mile Run.

This view of a Frick Park cabin (constructed in 1937) offers a view of the stonework and woodwork.

A Frick Park picnic area is shown in 1937.

A night game is in progress at the Frick Park lawn bowling green. The lawn bowling green was dedicated in 1932, probably at a different location, but it was operating at its current site by at least 1938. It is the only public lawn bowling green in Pennsylvania. Each of the two greens is a 120-foot square of carefully mowed, rolled, and gently watered grass that can accommodate eight games at one time. Improvements to this area made over the years were construction of the Bowling Green clubhouse (1938) and shelter (1940). The Frick Park Lawn Bowling Club maintains the greens.

The Pittsburgh Country Club area included tennis courts. During the planning process for the park, however, the decision was made to transfer recreational facilities to the outside edge of the park and to leave the central portion in a more natural state. By 1940, new tennis courts had been constructed near South Braddock Avenue. By 1942, the country club courts had been eliminated. This is a view of a "skating rink" created by flooding over the Braddock area tennis courts.

This is a view of Frick Park along Beechwood Boulevard, where the heavily used Blue Slide Playground is located today. By 1944, Frick Park included 457 acres, .4 miles of driveways, and 2 miles of walks. There were ten double tennis courts, nine nature trails, seven shelters, and one baseball field. The park is soon to be expanded by nearly 100 acres through addition of the Nine Mile Run Valley. The addition will link Frick Park with Summerset and connect it to the Monongahela River.

Eight

THE JEWISH COMMUNITY

The first Jews to move to Pittsburgh in any significant number arrived in the 1840s and settled downtown and in Old Allegheny. For the most part, these were German Jews, mainly businessmen. Burial societies and synagogues were established after more arrived from Europe. By 1910, the Hill District contained about 40,000 Jews. By this time, the Germans had been joined by immigrants from Lithuania, Hungary, Poland, Russia, Latvia, and Romania, driven here by the pogroms of 1881 and by Pittsburgh's status as the workshop of the world.

Rodef Shalom was the one of the first synagogues in Pittsburgh, establishing a congregation downtown in 1862. Along with synagogues, the Jewish community in Pittsburgh established many organizations to take care of their members. This included local branches of national organizations, such as the National Council of Jewish Women and the Hebrew Free Loan Association, in addition to local agencies, including the Gusky Orphanage, the House of Shelter, the Jewish Home for the Aged, and the Hebrew Institute. Montefiore Hospital was the only Jewish hospital in Pittsburgh. It was established so that Jewish patients would not have to eat nonkosher food, and Jewish doctors would have a place to practice medicine.

The Irene Kaufmann Settlement (IKS) began in the Hill District as a school and social service agency and became so popular over the years that it moved to larger quarters in Squirrel Hill. While it was still on Centre Avenue, the IKS provided a wealth of services to the community, with social clubs, classes in high-school courses and vocational courses, visiting nurse services, and physical education facilities. It was later supplanted by the Young Men's and Women's Hebrew Association (YMWHA) building in Oakland and, later, by the Jewish Community Center in Squirrel Hill.

By the 1930s, many of the Jews who had lived on the North Side, the Hill, and some of the small mill towns surrounding Pittsburgh moved east to Squirrel Hill. In most cases, their synagogues moved with them. Rodef Shalom moved to Shadyside and has always had a large membership from Squirrel Hill. Tree of Life moved to Oakland and then to Squirrel Hill. Poale Zedeck opened a Squirrel Hill location in addition to their original one on Grant Street.

This was and still is a very vibrant Jewish community. By the 1950s, Holocaust survivors moved to Squirrel Hill, and from the 1970s on, Jews from the former Soviet Union have added to that mix. Most of the outward signs of Jewish life in Squirrel Hill can be seen on Forbes and Murray Avenues. Today there are Jewish day schools, yeshivot for religious boys and girls, synagogues encompassing all variations of the spectrum, kosher food stores and restaurants, housing for Jewish seniors, and many other organizations too numerous to mention.

This is a photograph of the second Rodef Shalom temple, at Eighth Street near Penn Avenue in downtown Pittsburgh. The congregation was established in 1862 by members who had split off from Congregation Shaarai Shemaim. By 1901, the membership of Rodef Shalom had grown to 132, so a second and larger building was constructed on the same lot as the original. In Hebrew, Rodef Shalom means "seek peace."

In 1907, the congregation of Rodef Shalom moved to a larger building, located at 4905 Fifth Avenue in Shadyside. This building was designed by Henry Hornbostle, a renowned architect who also built many buildings at Carnegie Mellon University, the University of Pittsburgh, and the City-County Building downtown. Rodef Shalom is the largest Reform congregation in western Pennsylvania and is the oldest extant congregation in Pittsburgh.

This view of the main sanctuary of Rodef Shalom includes two of the stained-glass windows, the Kimball organ, the Eternal Light (Ner Tamid), and a glimpse of the magnificent stained-glass skylight. When the building was constructed, there was seating for 1,120 on the main floor, with an additional 350 seats in the balcony. There are currently more than 1,400 members who belong to the congregation.

A confirmation class from Rodef Shalom is pictured in 1911, when the Fifth Avenue building was four years old. Rabbi J. Leonard Levy stands in the center in front of the Ark of the Covenant. Levy was a dynamic leader of the congregation, and this new building was dedicated in his name.

The confirmation class of 1917 poses for a photographer at the Tree of Life congregation. Tree of Life (the Hebrew translation of Etz Hayim) was the second-oldest congregation in Pittsburgh and began when an Orthodox minority resigned from Rodef Shalom, which they considered too liberal. The members of Tree of Life met in various locations downtown before moving to Craft Avenue in Oakland in 1906.

This is a Tree of Life confirmation class from 1919, when they were still in their Oakland location. Daniel A. Crone was the architect for the Craft Avenue complex, which later housed the Pittsburgh Playhouse. In 1952, the congregation moved to an empty lot at the corner of Shady and Wilkins Avenues and built a new synagogue, where they are still located.

This is a current view of the Tree of Life synagogue.

A graduation class from Poale Zedeck Synagogue is pictured on June 20, 1948. Poale Zedeck, which means "workers of justice," was known as the Hungarian synagogue when it was formed in 1881. At that time, the Orthodox congregation rented space in a hall downtown on Grant Street. From there they moved to a house on Federal Street, and in 1901, a house on Crawford Street was purchased for a permanent location. In 1928, the congregation opened a second location on the corner of Phillips and Tilbury Streets, which now serves as their only place of worship.

This is an early postcard from the Irene Kaufmann Settlement, which grew out of a merger in 1895 between the Columbian Council and Rabbi Lippman Mayer's Russian School for Jewish immigrant children. The new organization was initially housed in a small room on Miller Street in the Hill District. After a few years in another location (at 32 Townsend Street), the Irene Kaufmann Settlement moved to the Slagel Homestead, at 1835 Centre Avenue.

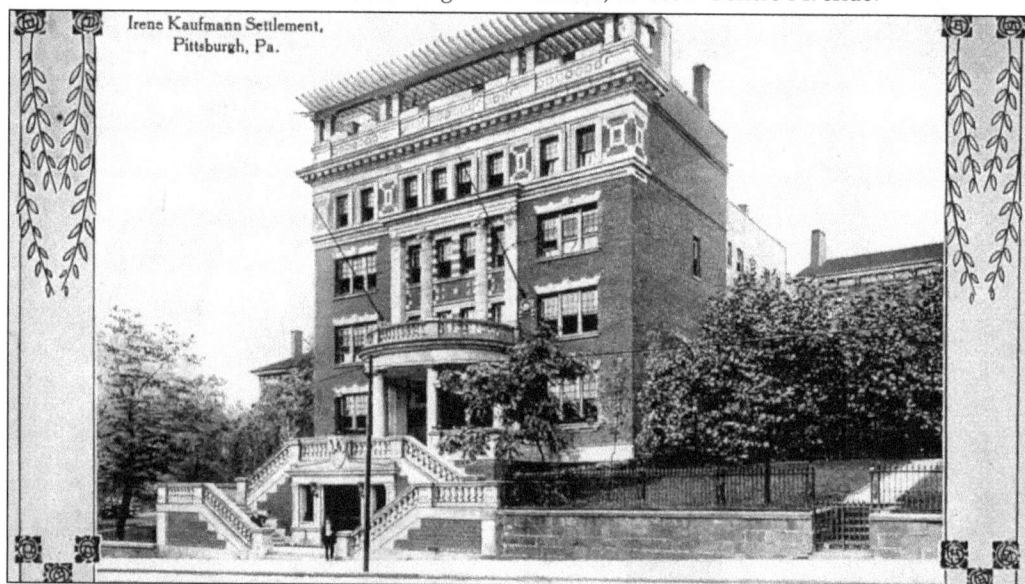

Irene Kaufmann Settlement,
Pittsburgh, Pa.

The Irene Kaufmann Settlement offered classes in the English language, music, art, chemistry, dressmaking, dancing, physics, and many other subjects. Social, religious, and political groups held their meetings there, and health and hygiene programs for the neighborhood were organized in 1901. So much activity was taking place at the settlement that they needed more space. In 1908, a new building was added to the facility in honor of Irene Kaufmann, with funds donated by her parents.

In 1910, a group of 16 men formed the Young Men's Hebrew Association (YMHA), and in 1925, the Young Men's and Women's Hebrew Association (YMWHA) moved into a new building at 315 Bellefield Avenue in Oakland. This building contained the Morris Kaufmann Auditorium, a swimming pool, a gymnasium, and other recreational facilities. Plays and concerts were held there at a time when the Jewish population was moving farther away from the Hill and downtown.

Rabbi Aaron M. Ashinsky helped create the Jewish Home for the Aged in Pittsburgh in 1906. The original home was on Brackenridge Avenue in the Hill. By 1933, the home had become overcrowded, despite two additions, so they moved to a 17-acre tract in Squirrel Hill (shown here), where the old Brown estate had been. The facility was renamed the Riverview Center for Jewish Seniors in 1980.

Beth Shalom (meaning "house of peace") is shown at its location at Shady Avenue and Beacon Street. The Conservative congregation was established in 1918 by a group of eastern European Jews. These founding families held services in a space above the Orpheum Theater (near Forbes and Murray Avenues) and called themselves the Squirrel Hill Congregation. By 1922, the membership had grown too large for their rented space, so they built the new synagogue with seating for 1,400.

The original Squirrel Hill building of Beth Shalom was expanded in 1931 to create a larger main sanctuary. This is a photograph of the expanded building prior to more recent changes, including reconstruction of a portion of the improvements after a 1997 fire.

Here is a graduation picture of the Beth Shalom Religious School in the summer of 1932. The gentleman in the front row, seated between the two young women, is Rabbi Goodman Rose, who served the congregation from 1924 until 1950.

The Agency for Jewish Learning, formerly known as the Jewish Education Institute (JEI), is currently housed at 2740 Beechwood Boulevard in the former rectory of the St. Philomena parish. Prior to the move in 1996, the JEI and the Hebrew Institute were located at 6401 Forbes Avenue. The agency serves as a resource for Jewish education throughout Pittsburgh by providing training, consultation, and collaborative learning opportunities for Jewish educators and institutions.

This is a Beechwood Boulevard view of Community Day, a school located at the corner of Beechwood Boulevard and Forward Avenue next to the Agency for Jewish Learning. Community Day is the only Conservative Jewish day school in the city. Classes are offered to children from kindergarten through the eighth grade. The school began in 1972 in the Hebrew Institute building, at Forbes and Denniston, and offered classes for children from kindergarten through the third grade.

Temple Sinai was founded in 1946, and the synagogue was dedicated in 1949 at the corner of Forbes Avenue and Murdoch Street. The Reform synagogue constructed its building as an addition to the Worthington mansion. In 1969, the sanctuary was constructed. In 1993, the chapel and religious school were renovated. This photograph shows Rabbi Aaron B. Ilson speaking to a group at the groundbreaking ceremony for the religious school and auditorium in 1956.

Nine

RETAIL AND HIGHWAY DEVELOPMENT

The electric streetcar line that began running up Forbes Avenue from Schenley Park to Murray Avenue and on to Homestead in 1893 spurred both retail and residential development. Retail development began on Forbes and Murray Avenues, extending eastward and southward from the Forbes-Murray intersection. When it became apparent that Murray Avenue would become a commercial street and would lose its original residential character, storerooms were squeezed into what was originally front yards of those homes. Murray Avenue was the location for all the produce, meat, and service stores. Forbes Avenue became the center for clothing, shoes, and banking.

To this day, Forbes and Murray Avenues represent the retail and cultural heart of Squirrel Hill. The uniqueness of the Squirrel Hill retail establishment is its survival through extensive retail business changes that have occurred in America since World War II. Its 1930-style retail characteristics remain. The neighborhood has survived the automobile. It is very walkable, and you can still count on meeting an acquaintance every time you shop, stroll, or seek a cup of coffee or tea.

Although Squirrel Hill was largely built up by the late 1940s, the neighborhood faced additional change in the 1950s with the construction of the Squirrel Hill Tunnel and the Parkway East. That construction changed the terrain on the south end of Squirrel Hill and eliminated a number of streets, houses, and schools. However, the new road, with direct access to Murray Avenue, also increased Squirrel Hill's access to other parts of the city and brought substantial new traffic into the area. The tunnel and parkway are prominent features in today's Squirrel Hill.

This view, looking south in 1927, shows the 1700 block of Murray Avenue from the intersection of Forbes Avenue. The Manor Theater, which exists today, is on the left. In 1935, Gulf Oil built the second-largest gas station in the country on the corner lot in the foreground. That station existed into the late 1990s. It has been replaced with a three-story retail complex erected in 2004 and containing a Rite-Aid drugstore.

In 1932, we see a closer view of the Manor Theater. The Tudor style of architecture has been maintained to this day. The upper floor is now home to Barnes & Noble booksellers, and the Manor Theater has been expanded to four screens.

At Klein's Delicatessen, located at 1716 Murray Avenue, a blue-plate special is offered for 50¢ in 1932. In these few blocks of Murray Avenue, there were 26 stores that sold food. Grocers, butchers, and bakers were side-by-side with businesses selling fruit, fish, and poultry. Each store had its own clientele. These stores preceded the era of supermarkets. In 1940, an A&P opened on Murray Avenue.

The area of 1718–1720 Murray Avenue is pictured in 1932. Ben Little's Shoe Store is in the foreground. (Little's moved to the middle of the Forbes business district and today is the largest quality shoe store in Pittsburgh.) Typical of storefronts at this time is generous use of plate glass for display of goods and carrara glass decorating the storefronts. Note the sidewalk metal doors, which accessed store basements. These are still used today all along Murray Avenue.

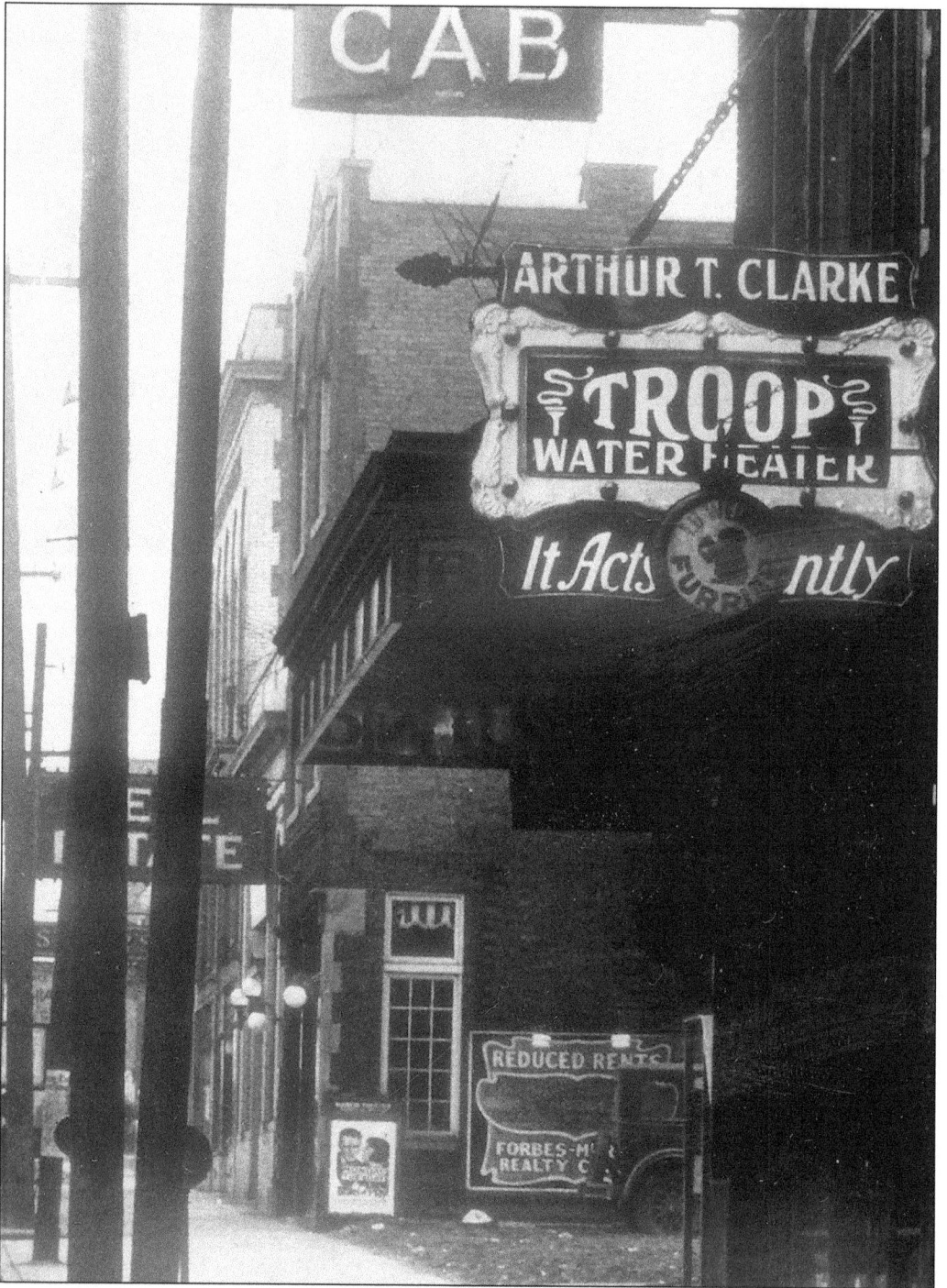

This view shows the long block on Forbes Avenue from Murray to Shady Avenues in 1927. This area was the other developing commercial center of Squirrel Hill. By 1940, there were over 20 modern businesses on this block. Newman's (a clothing store), Little's (a shoe store), Franklin (a bank), Moser's (a furniture store), Rosen's (a drugstore), and Isaly's (a delicatessen) were representative of this era. There were few gaps left on Forbes to fill.

This parade marks the official opening of the extension of Forbes Avenue from Dallas Avenue to Pittsburgh's eastern boundary at Braddock Avenue on October 28, 1926. Frick Park is on the right, and Homewood Cemetery is on the left. These two institutions remain intact today and provide the boundary to commercial development along this strip. Other than removal of the trolley tracks, this is how Forbes Avenue looks today.

This view looks up Murray Avenue from Darlington Road in 1937. In the background is the tower of the Sixth Presbyterian Church. On the near corner is the Manor Drug Store, and behind the utility pole is the marquee of the Manor Theater. The Great Depression is at an end, and these late-model cars suggest Squirrel Hill is sharing in the recovery. By the late 1930s, there were four movie theaters: the Manor, Beacon, Squirrel Hill, and Orpheum. The Manor and Squirrel Hill remain today.

This state-of-the-art station was built in 1935 on the corner of Forbes and Shady Avenues by the Atlantic Refining Company. It has motorized gas pumps and an outdoor hydraulic car lift. Kamin Chevrolet surrounds the gas station. By 1941, there were six car dealers on Forbes and Murray Avenues. In 1935, Samson Buick was offering a new Buick coupe for $615. The post–World War II automotive boom quickly forced them to the suburbs for more space.

Forbes and Shady Avenues are seen in a view looking toward Murray Avenue in 1941. In the foreground is the same station shown in the previous picture. In this view, a second gas station (Amoco) has been built next to this Atlantic refining station. Gas stations occupied three of the four corners at this intersection from after World War II into the 1980s.

This photograph was taken in 1971 during construction of the Carnegie Library, at the intersection of Forbes and Murray Avenue across from the Sixth Presbyterian Church. A public parking garage was also built at ground level. The Asbury Methodist Church was previously located at this site. A major renovation in 2004–2005 was designed to give the library an expanded and more visible presence in Squirrel Hill.

The Morrowfield Hotel complex is shown here in 1937. At the end of World War I, Thomas Watkins (a major real-estate developer) and several Squirrel Hill businessmen had a large vision. They conceived of a community within a community. The Morrowfield complex (bounded by Forward, Murray, Shady, and Morrowfield Avenues) included numerous apartment houses, retail shops, a parking garage, a bowling alley, an 800-seat theater, and one large 148-unit hotel and apartment building.

Completed in 1923, the Morrowfield was one of the city's best. Celebrities and entertainers such as Fanny Brice, Al Jolson, Alfred Lunt, Lynn Fontanne, and the Marx brothers stayed here. Before completion of the parkway and tunnels, the Morrowfield had a picturesque view of the valley.

In this 1921 view, the old wooden Beechwood Boulevard Bridge has been demolished to prepare for a new bridge. Visitors from the nearby areas south of the park had no easy access. Even today, Pocusset Street is narrow and difficult once it leaves the Squirrel Hill neighborhood. The view is from Schenley Park and shows the Saline Street ravine that snaked through the tree-filled valley.

The new Beechwood Boulevard Bridge connects Schenley Park and Greenfield. It was completed in 1923, providing a grand entrance over a branch of Four Mile Run. The great white arch and its decorations shone brightly above Saline Street. Beechwood Boulevard was created from a collection of streets widened into a fashionable upscale carriage way in the early days of automobiles.

Pittsburgh is a city of bridges, and the Squirrel Hill neighborhood has its share. Atop the basic arch of the new Beechwood Boulevard Bridge, Roush, the architect, added ornamental bronze and cut Indiana limestone, sculptured lampposts, pedestals, urns, and inscribed pylons. Today, the Parkway East (built in the early 1950s) passes under this bridge.

This is a 1950 construction photograph of the Commercial Street Bridge. The view features the eastern entrance of the Squirrel Hill Tunnel (upper left) and the three-arched Commercial Street Bridge over Nine Mile Run. This is the Parkway East, which opened in 1953 (after World War II had delayed the building of the tunnel, bridges, and roadway). Growth of the eastern suburbs was under way in the 1950s, and this artery also eased traffic on the streets of Squirrel Hill.

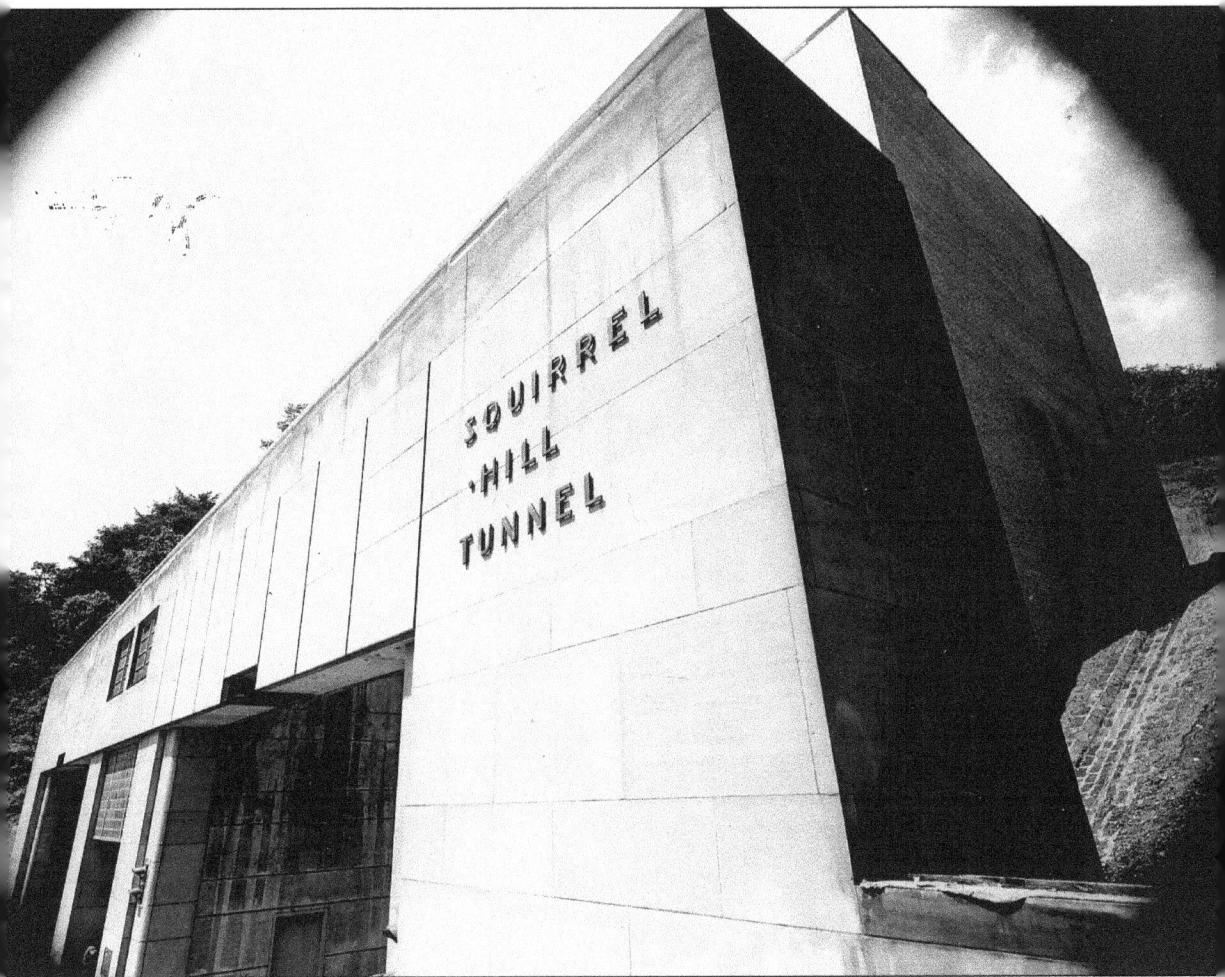

The west entrance of the Squirrel Hill Tunnel is shown in May 1953. Two separate two-lane tubes form the tunnel. The tunnel is 4,225 feet long and cost $18 million—the largest sum the Pennsylvania Department of Transportation had spent on any single project to date.

Taken in May 1953, this photograph of the Squirrel Hill Tunnel shows the Morrowfield apartment building in the background. The opening was a major celebration. Squirrel Hill's Taylor Allderdice High School band was a significant participant in this dedication of the Penn-Lincoln Parkway (Interstate 376), known today as the Parkway East.

The first cars pass through the tunnel during the dedication of the Squirrel Hill Tunnel on June 5, 1953. Although this narrative ends with the opening of the tunnel, the history of the Squirrel Hill community continues to unfold.

www.ingramcontent.com/pod-product-compliance
Lightning Source LLC
Chambersburg PA
CBHW050557110426
42813CB00008B/2380